Sweet Paris

A love affair with Parisian pastries, chocolates and desserts

WRITTEN & PHOTOGRAPHED BY

MICHAEL PAUL

hardie grant books

MELBOURNE · LONDON

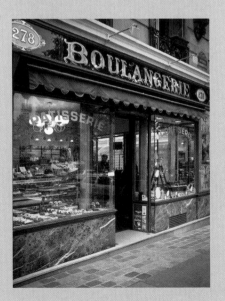

Contents

I love Paris

I fell in love with Paris long before I ever went there. It was at the tender age of fourteen growing up on the other side of the world, in a small Southern Hemisphere city. There I was sent to Miss Nichols' dance classes to learn some social graces and etiquette. Having spent most of my adolescence at austere, male-only boarding schools, this was my first close encounter with the opposite sex. Hair slicked with my father's pomade, I nervously clutched the perspiring hands of spotty girls smelling of cheap shampoo, and ungainly attempted to trip the light fantastic. From the first lesson it was glaringly apparent that Miss Nichols had only one record, the classic Cole Porter song 'I Love Paris'. We learnt to waltz, fox trot, strip the willow and, god forbid, even the Gay Gordon to the whimsical strains of Ella Fitzgerald's rendition of this timeless song with its starry-eyed orchestration. Did I care? Hell no! I was in seventh heaven. Something magic had happened – I had discovered girls. And 'I Love Paris' had become the soundtrack to this adolescent hormonal upsurge. From then on, I loved Paris too. In my fantasies it was a city of romance, glamorous fashion models and amorous adventures; a city where you fell in love…

Many years later, and now living in London, I went on my first visit to Paris and the love affair was rekindled. With a hunger for knowledge and hedonism, I made a two-handed grab to pack away all the pleasures Paris had to offer. Frequent trips ensued but I soon realised that to really know Paris I had to avoid being a conspicuous tourist armed with a guidebook, ticking off its attractions one by one. Instead, to get intimately acquainted with the French capital, I had to become part of the fabric of the city, to meld into the background, to find the forgotten places, the covert cracks, that are unknown to visitors and often to its citizens too. With this desire for anonymity and a love of sauntering through the Paris streets I became a *flâneur* – the French term for a stroller or loiterer. The Parisian dandy and poet Charles Baudelaire described a *flâneur* as 'a person who walks the city in order to experience it'. Lured by Paris's seductive backstreets and mysterious passageways, I meandered anonymously, with no apparent purpose, in search of adventure and creative stimulation.

Denizens of Paris will tell you it is a city meant to be seen on foot. The only way to take in its wealth of detail and distractions is to walk its length and breadth.

It is said that Paris is dominated by its triumphant landmarks and classical monuments but, as a photographer, the Paris I love is defined by its details. God is most certainly in the minutiae rather than its grandiose statements.

But don't get me wrong – like many, I am in awe of its sweeping vistas, distant perspectives, flamboyant architecture and its glorious orchestration of geometry. Few cities can boast such splendour. There is also a side of me that is fascinated by the French sense of order: the faultless symmetry, the topiary trees like troops on parade, the imperial lines of its avenues, row upon row of indistinguishable lampposts, lengthy cloisters with identical arches, the matching park benches. All testimony to a well-tended formal face designed by visionaries like Napolean III and his sidekick Baron Haussmann.

But it's the countless intriguing details of Paris that captivate my camera. Gold railings, elegant typefaces, belle époque decoration, elaborate entrances, carved stone faces, ornate ironwork, street signs, stairways, lace curtains, café chairs – there is an object to appease every appetite. And, talking of appetites, the itinerant *flâneur* gets hungry. Very hungry! Irrepressible cravings to satisfy a lust for something sweet drove me into the cafés, tea salons, chocolate shops and patisseries that abound in Paris like no other city on this earth. The more I roamed the streets, the greater my passion for the pastries, chocolates and desserts of Paris became. A new love affair had begun – a love of sweet Paris.

Apart from being utterly delectable, the pastries, cakes and chocolates in this town look the part too; an allure that continues to hold me, as a photographer of food, in its thrall. Not only a global fashion and cultural centre, Paris is also the sweet-toothed capital of the world with chic chocolate leading the way. Paris's profile has been raised by the annual *Salon du Chocolat*, an event that celebrates its prowess as the city of cacao. But the French chocolate revolution has also benefited from a shift in attitude whereby chocolate has taken on a new, more desirable mantle as the hip, high-octane food of the *haut monde* – and as luck would have it, French politicians too. But, most of all, chocolate in the hands of the Parisian elite *maîtres chocolatiers* has become sublime in its simplest expression, and delightfully outrageous in its extreme examples. Equally, Paris's pastries are in the same league. Gastronomic gods like Pierre Hermé have taken gâteaux and desserts to new heights of desire and deliciousness, whereas the celebrated time-honoured tea salons still seduce sybarites from the four corners of the globe.

The city's countless purveyors of sweet confections display a level of technique and skill that only the French can achieve. Yet these delicacies remain infinitely affordable. Whereas many visitors, as well as local Parisians, are priced out of the haute cuisine restaurants, luckily most of us can afford a couple of euros for a mouth-watering *macaron*. Even a decadent chocolate *éclair*, *millefeuille* or *Mont Blanc* from the best pâtisserie is within most people's price range. These edible art forms are exhibited like glistening gems in their windows. But have you ever wondered what is in all those luscious creamy pastries or in that dizzying array of chocolates? Probably like me you have found yourself drooling, nose pressed against the window of a neighbourhood pâtisserie or chocolate shop, unable to decide what to buy? So in '*Sweet Paris*' I try to describe what they are, tell you a bit about their origins, the essential ingredients and how they are made. And with some trepidation I offer up some suggestions as to who makes among the best in Paris. There is also a selection of traditional French recipes, so you can try out these glamorous goodies at home. But, be aware gentle reader, this book is not intended as a guide or directory but rather a light-hearted look at the sweet pleasures of Paris for your delectation. It is a celebration of the chocolates, classic cakes, pastries and desserts that have become part of everyday life in the French capital. Although I include some of my favourite addresses, it is by no means a complete list – look upon it instead as a tantalising *flânerie* through the streets of temptation that are Sweet Paris.

1

The Chocolate Capital of the World

·····································

Riding the wave of a new style of sublime chocolate created by its exclusive avant-garde chocolatiers, Paris is now the world capital of all things cacao. No longer in the shadow of Belgium and Switzerland, French chocolates are perceived as exciting, dark, intense, cutting-edge and, dare I say it, almost healthy. Wishful thinking, perhaps, but it may have something to do with the fact that the French use less cream and sugar in their chocolates. True or false, nonetheless it's a reputation that has stuck.

The new chocolate idols have gained cult status as accomplished artists, not just artisans. Along with the brigade of top chefs and *pâtissiers*, the *maîtres chocolatiers* have become the darlings of the press – the Paris rock stars of today who have added a new panache and ganache to what was once a bit of a cultural backwater. Their popularity has helped put Paris back on the world foodie map as the ultimate destination for those with a sweet tooth and a *joie de vivre*.

Paris's new wave of stellar *maîtres chocolatiers* such as Patrick Roger, Pierre Hermé, Franck Kestener and Jacques Genin have shown scant regard for the classic approach, overtaking the more traditional yet nonetheless excellent artisanal makers such as Jean-Paul Hévin, Michel Cluizel, Christian Constant and Michel Chaudun.

Patrick Roger's witty, flippant and often risqué chocolate sculptures – everything from gorillas and penguins to nude rugby players – have been the tittle-tattle of Paris and seem to become all the more outlandish in the peak chocolate seasons. Arguably this is all part of his unswerving mission to create the finest chocolate in all of France. On the other hand the traditionalists sculpt with more predictable themes like the Eiffel tower. This all suggests that aesthetics play a big part in the experience. Jewel-like displays of *bonbons* and other edible works of art in the windows of these inventive chocolatiers tempt even the strong-willed, despite the price which often matches the exclusivity of their creations.

The craze for chic chocolate shows no sign of letting up. New shops open every week in Paris's posh *arrondissements*. Allegedly there are more chocolate shops in the City of Light than in any other city in Europe – over 300 are listed in the phone directory. This proliferation includes the high-end *maîtres chocolatiers*, *pâtissiers* and gourmet food stores as well as popular chains such as La Maison du Chocolat, L'Atelier du Chocolat and literally hundreds of smaller independent chocolatiers and *confiseurs*. It all goes to underline that in a modern-day culture slavish to sweetness, Paris has earned the right to be crowned the chocolate capital of the world.

∾

Chocolate Bars

〜

True connoisseurs of chocolate focus on chocolate rather than chocolates – in other words, bars and not filled chocolates, or *bonbons*. They believe that the bar is the purest, most concentrated form of real chocolate, while *bonbons* fall into the realm of 'candy chocolate'. Purists talk of chocolate as though it was wine, and use the same flowery vocabulary – nutty, spicy, fruity, etc – to describe it.

A high-quality chocolate bar is usually made up of cocoa, sugar, cocoa butter, vanilla and lecithin (in short, vegetable fats) as an emulsifier. Bars can be made in two different ways: direct from the bean or from *couvertures* – chocolate that is melted and sometimes blended to create a new chocolate.

For devotees, the quality of the cacao beans used, where they come from and their vintage, along with the percentage of cocoa solids, is what really matters – 65% seems about the cut-off point and anything above this is desirable. The origin of the beans noticeably influences the quality of the chocolate made from them. Some of the best beans come from Venezuela, Peru, Costa Rica, Madagascar and Bolivia.

If all of this fills you with trepidation, fear not! There are easy solutions for finding the best chocolate in Paris. The first thing you can do is go on a chocolate-tasting tour with an expert like the highly knowledgeable blogger, author and fervent foodie David Lebovitz. Or, for the real enthusiast, you can participate in one of the chocolate classes or tours of the very finest chocolate in town with Paris's high priestess of chocolate, Chloé Doutre-Roussel – the most passionate chocolate champion on this planet. Choco-Chloé, as she is known to her friends, will enthral you with her infectious excitement and generously share her vast knowledge of her cherished subject. She also sells online the exclusive *El Ceibo* range of chocolate bars from Bolivia, and, for serious chocolate lovers, her exquisite Chloé bars of intense chocolate which she partners with a blend of her own tea.

If time prevents such a delightful excursion then you should make a beeline for the pre-eminent chocolatiers in town. But, be warned, many just sell single origin bars – melted, tempered, moulded chocolate from a supplier that shows no creativity. To avoid this, my first choice would be to visit the 'wild child of chocolate', Patrick Roger, in Saint-Germain. His blocks of chocolate are fashioned from some of the finest cacao sources on this earth. Others who do 'plantation bars' (which use beans from a specific plantation, a bit like a domaine for wines) are Jacques Genin, François Pralus, Michel Cluizel and Jean-Paul Hévin. And as a slight odd-ball in the mix with its own cult following you could try a bar of Bernachon from Lyon, available only at the fairy-tale *confiserie* L'Étoile d'Or in Montmartre.

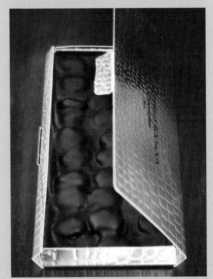

Bonbons

⁓

Filled chocolates, or *bonbons* as they are called in France, cover a multitude of sinful delights. Whereas purists consider these lesser forms of chocolate we all know that they probably secretly desire them as much as we do. Of course we have to be clear on what we mean by 'filled chocolates' as these days nearly anything sweet or savoury and covered in chocolate is labelled a 'chocolate'. In the main, though, we are talking about the bastions of filled chocolate-making. These include *pralinés* (not to be confused with the Belgian 'pralines', without the accent, used to describe any filled chocolates), ganaches and chocolates filled with marzipan. But I guess, to the chagrin of those purists, we must also delve into the realm of candy chocolates, filled with caramel, fudge and cream. And, of course, we should mention *mendiants* – small medals of chocolate decorated with dried fruits and nuts. Chocolate truffles are different again – balls of creamy ganache sometimes coated in an outer layer of chocolate and rolled in cocoa powder. In short these are the main types of chocolates you will find in the plethora of chocolatiers in Paris, whose bulging counters display a vast selection of filled treats – flavoured with everything from liquorice and coffee to herbs and liqueurs.

As a lay chocolate person, I'm completely in awe of the skills, imagination and creativity of the top Parisian master chocolatiers who craft these demanding creations, which combine astonishing flavours with the complexity and sensitivity of chocolate. It takes an accomplished alchemist, as well as artist, to know how the *couverture* coating will taste with the filling. They need the nose of a perfumer and the palate of a sommelier to discover those harmonious blends of aromas and ingredients that send your senses soaring into space.

So who sells the best bonbons in Paris? The clear winner is again Patrick Roger, whose sensorial sensations are the talk of the town. When he is not racing his powerful Italian motorcycle along the city's boulevards or in search of exotic ingredients, he can be found in his kitchens creating his innovative assortment of unconventionally flavoured chocolates: every one disguising a unique complexity of taste and texture that expresses his passion and expertise as one of France's finest. He is obsessed with the quality of the ingredients he uses, which in many cases he makes or grows himself. Yet there is nothing ostentatious in what he does. Unlike others, both he and his highly contemporary take on chocolate remain very approachable. I am a big fan of his 'Fantasy' chocolate filled with Orinoco tonka beans and a very vanillary caramel, and also his 'Savage' – smooth, soft caramel flavoured with verbena and yuzu, a type of citrus fruit from Japan. Who else comes close? The multi-talented and brilliant Pierre Hermé for one. His flavour combinations and contrasting textures are also in a league of their own. And the highly accomplished chocolatier Jacques Genin must be on your list: his high temple to taste in the Marais stocks some of the best *bonbons* in the business.

PARISIAN CHOCOLATE TRUFFLES

I can't see the point in making filled chocolates. It's a painstaking, big-girl's-blouse of a business, and they will never be as perfect as those made by a skilled Parisian chocolatier. Chocolate truffles are more my style. They are fun to make and not too difficult. They make an ideal gift as well as a delectable after-dinner indulgence. You can also add rum, ginger or any number of flavours, but personally I like them unencumbered by booze.

. . . .

MAKES ABOUT 25–30

250 g (9 oz) bittersweet dark chocolate
125 ml (4½ fl oz/½ cup) double (heavy) cream
1 vanilla pod

FOR THE COATING
200 g (7 oz) milk chocolate
2 tablespoons good-quality cocoa powder

Finely chop the chocolate with a knife and place in a heatproof mixing bowl.

Pour the cream into a medium saucepan. Use a small knife to split the vanilla pod lengthways and scrape out the seeds, then add them to the cream along with the pod and bring to the boil.

When boiling, remove immediately from the heat and take out the vanilla pod. Pour through a strainer into the chopped chocolate. Whisk to combine the chocolate and cream in a circular movement until the mixture is smooth.

Leave to cool but don't refrigerate. When the ganache mixture is firm, warm through over a saucepan of simmering water, then whisk the mixture until creamy.

Cover a large baking tray with parchment paper. Scoop out dollops of ganache and roll into walnut-sized balls. Place on the tray and refrigerate until hard. In the meantime, prepare the coating. Place the chocolate in a heatproof bowl and place on top of a saucepan filled with about 5 cm (2 inches) water, making sure that the bottom of the bowl is not touching the water. Allow the chocolate to melt slowly.

As soon as it has melted, turn off the heat, remove the bowl from the pan and wrap a clean tea towel round the base to keep it warm. Stir until it cools to 30–31°C. Use a chocolate thermometer to check and once it reaches this temperature, it's ready to use.

Place the cocoa powder in a shallow bowl. Remove the truffles from the refrigerator and, using chopsticks or a fork, dip them into the melted milk chocolate and then roll them immediately in cocoa powder. Set aside until completely hard.

2

Paris – A Taste for Fashion

....

Paris has a thirst for fashion like no other city on earth. Since the Middle Ages it has been a place of ideas and inspiration, setting trends not just in France but across the globe. Today its fashion designers continue to dominate the world of *haute couture* while the city's architects, product and industrial designers have achieved international acclaim.

This appetite for innovation means that fashions and fads come and go in Paris faster than a TGV train. As the novelist Honoré de Balzac observed, 'The Parisian is interested in everything and, in the end, interested in nothing'. Fickle as they may seem, the Paris population's desire for novelty, distraction and pleasure seems insatiable. New restaurants open every day while just as many close. Boutiques, bars, tearooms and cafés spring up in every chic arrondissement and the once no-go quartiers suddenly become hip places to live or hang out.

Riding high on the fashion and passion for the sweet pleasures of Paris, the craze for chocolate and the mania for *macarons* has reached epic proportions, fuelled by the 30 million-plus tourists who visit the capital each year – making it the most visited city in the world. Its celebrated *salons de thé*, such as Ladurée and Angelina, continue to be among the main draws, as do its chocolate shops, pâtisseries and gourmet food stores. The fascination with these hip foods may well be fed by the intimate relationship with haute couture: sweet treats regularly appear on the catwalk, where models can be seen daubed in dripping chocolate or sporting strategically placed *macarons*. Pundits will tell you more *macarons* are munched during Paris fashion week than at any other time of the year; so much so that Pierre Hermé sells a box branded 'Make-Up Artist', and couriers ply to and fro Paris's top pâtisseries ferrying boxes of these vivid-coloured confections backstage at the main collections.

Driven by the need for novelty, new pastry or dessert fashions make their debut on a regular basis in shop windows of the most inventive purveyors of Paris's sweet pleasures. In addition to the universally modish *macaron*, old-style meringues are making a comeback and the robust American brownie has now gained a firm foothold. But perhaps the most surprising success has been the invasion of the cupcake. In a chauvinistic city resistant to anything non-French, the sight of outrageously decorated, 'in-yo-face', Yankee-doodle-dandy cupcakes popping up everywhere in Paris is unexpected to say the least. And, while on the subject of influences from across the pond, another revelation in recent years has been the growing popularity of a new style of marshmallow, or *guimauve*, in France which luckily bears scant resemblance to its sugary, uninspiring American cousin.

❧

Macarons

~

Le macaron has become emblematic of the French fashion for fun, frivolous confectionery. Chic, feminine and irresistible, it is the ultimate *amuse-bouche* – a creamy, crumbly mouthful of sheer indulgent decadence.

The name 'macaroon' – or *macaron* as it should be correctly spelt to distinguish it from those rather cloying coconut macaroons that my mum used to make – derives from the Italian word *maccarone*, which in turn probably comes from the verb *ammaccare*, meaning to crush (referring to the almond flour which is the basic ingredient). Similar to a meringue, it is made from a mixture of egg whites, ground almonds, and both granulated and icing sugar. Unlike a meringue, it is characterised by its smooth, flat dome; irregular circumference termed the 'foot'; and its flat base.

There has been much speculation about its origins. Although the name comes from Italian it is more than likely a French invention. 'Larousse Gastronomique' mentions *le macaron* as being created in 1791 in a convent in central France; others credit its first French appearance to Catherine de' Medici's Italian pastry chef, whom she brought with her to France in 1533 when she married Henry II. This, of course, would make it Italian… But these stories are often clouded in contradiction, with national pride playing its part. What we do know for a fact is that things kicked off in real style at the start of the twentieth century, when Pierre Desfontaines, the second cousin of Louis Ernest Ladurée, took two macaron shells and sandwiched them together with a delicious filling of chocolate ganache. Bravo Monsieur Desfontaines. Originally called the *'Gerbet'* or the *'Paris macaron'*, this heavenly marriage remains to this day the mainstay and symbol of Ladurée's success. A visit to one of the beautifully elegant tea salons of Ladurée in Paris is a must for every acolyte. You can excuse the slightly off-beat service when immersed in a world of fantasy which they have adorned with beautiful packaging and added value through glamorous imagery.

Le macaron is now as ubiquitous in Paris as the Eiffel Tower and my partner is somewhat of a connoisseur, having sampled literally hundreds of macarons since she started going to Paris as a fashion buyer many years back. Her penchant is for the *macarons* in a giddy array of colours and flavours from Fauchon – that bastion of fine French foodstuffs in the Place de la Madeleine – and it is hard to fault her choice. But for the ultimate hedonistic *macaron* experience, which will leave the palate pulsating with pleasure, try the delights that are to be found at Maison Pierre Hermé. Orgasmic – there is no other word for it. His satisfyingly crisp yet moist macarons filled with succulent, buttery ganaches and creams exquisitely flavoured to perfection are downright wanton and utterly seductive. Resistance is futile.

MOCHA MACARONS

This is a traditional French recipe for mouth-watering macarons with a few little extras to give them that je ne sais quoi. Making macarons is not as difficult as it seems. Getting the consistency of the macaron mix right is important, so that it settles within a few seconds when you pipe it out to smooth buttons. If it's too thick, add a little more egg white; too thin, then let it stand for a while before trying again. Being a macaron glutton I love mine fat and full of filling so I tend to overfill them, but the choice is yours as to how much ganache you use. Be sure to carefully sift your ingredients, a few times if necessary. Lumps are a definite no-no. And one last tip: always eat them at room temperature.

MAKES ABOUT 15

100 g (3½ oz) ground
   almonds
100 g (3½ oz) icing
   (confectioner's) sugar
2 tablespoons unsweetened
   cocoa powder
3 egg whites, at room
   temperature
100 g (3½ oz) granulated
   sugar
1 teaspoon instant coffee

*FOR THE GANACHE
FILLING*
125 g (4½ oz) bittersweet
   dark chocolate
60 ml (2 fl oz) double (heavy)
   cream
2 tablespoons coffee liqueur
   (such as Kahlua or Tia
   Maria)

Preheat the oven to 180°C/350°F/gas mark 4. Line a large baking sheet with a double layer of parchment paper. In a blender or food processor mix together the ground almonds, icing (confectioner's) sugar and cocoa powder, then sift into a large bowl to remove any lumps and set aside.

In another large mixing bowl, beat the egg whites until the peaks hold their shape. Continue whipping for about 2 minutes, adding in the granulated sugar and instant coffee, until very stiff and firm.

Gently fold in the ground almond mixture with a spatula until smooth and there is no sign of the egg whites, then scrape into a piping bag fitted with a 1 cm (½ inch) plain round tip. Pipe 30 or so 3 cm (1 inch) round mounds – about a tablespoon each of batter – roughly 3 cm (1 inch) apart, on to the parchment sheets. Tap the baking sheet a few times on the work surface to flatten the macarons and get rid of any air bubbles, then bake them for 15 minutes. Let cool completely and remove from the baking sheet.

To make the filling, finely chop the chocolate with a knife and place in a heatproof mixing bowl. Pour the double cream into a medium saucepan and bring to the boil. Remove from the heat, add the coffee liqueur, pour over the chocolate and whisk to combine in a circular movement until smooth.

Leave to cool but don't refrigerate. When cool, spoon into a piping bag with a plain or fluted 1.5 cm (¾ inch) nozzle and pipe the ganache on the inside of one of the macarons then sandwich together with another. Continue until all the macarons have been used up.

Let them stand at least half a day before eating to blend the flavours.

Pierre Hermé

～

The legendary Pierre Hermé is indisputably the most creative and gifted pastry chef in all of Paris – a true artist in every sense. He deserves more than the mention he gets here not because he was the youngest man ever to be named France's Pastry Chef of the Year, or because he has been awarded the *Chevalier de la Légion d'Honneur*, the highest civilian decoration in France, but because he is an out-and-out genius. Over the years the man has had many monikers bestowed by the press. The 'Picasso of Pastry', 'An Architect of Emotions' or the 'Dior of Desserts' are just a few of the flattering metaphors that have extolled his talents.

Probably most famous for his delectable macarons, he is also a master chocolatier-cum-*confiseur* and the architect of his own contemporary pastry creations and desserts, all renowned for their joyous and sometimes bizarre flavour marriages, which have become his signature. His skills lie in combining a cacophony of flavours and aromas that no one has associated before. Who would think of marrying asparagus and hazelnut oil in a macaron? But he also understands better than anyone that complementary textures are just as important as combining flattering flavours.

Monsieur Hermé began his illustrious career at the age of fourteen as apprentice to the legendary Gaston Lenôtre, the founding father of contemporary patisserie, whom he claims is his greatest mentor. At 24, he became the head pastry chef at Fauchon, where he remained for eleven years. Then, as vice-president at Ladurée, he had carte blanche to create all their products – *pâtisserie*, *viennoisserie* and chocolate – and develop a chain of luxury pastry shops. In 1998, he started his own business, Pierre Hermé Paris, with a boutique in Tokyo. His first Paris shop opened in 2002 in the rue Bonaparte, where, in the daily queue outside, you are likely to rub shoulders with fashion models, film directors, dot.com entrepreneurs, rock stars, oil magnates, aristocrats and be-minked, bejewelled Russian heiresses, all clamouring for his chocolate bonbons, perfect pastries or brimming boxes of *macarons*. It is all too easy to forget a million-dollar contract that includes a clause about your waistline when faced with the temptations that wait within the hallowed walls of Maison Pierre Hermé.

A classic enticement is his divine caramel *macaron* with a buttery *fleur de sel* caramel cream, resulting in the most perfect sensory sensation. His fashionable favourite remains the '*Ispahan*', a large rose *macaron* biscuit filled with fresh raspberries and rose petal cream flavoured with lychee. If this was the last thing I tasted on this earth I'd die a happy man. Chocoholics should try his *Plaisirs Sucrés*, a harmonious symphony that combines dacquoise biscuit, crunchy hazelnuts, thin wafers of milk chocolate ganache and milk chocolate Chantilly. Naturally his perfectly blended speciality chocolate bonbons are in a class of their own; the *Croquants au Praliné* are modern-day masterpieces of texture and taste, as are the *Assortiment de Chocolats au Macaron*.

A household name in France, Pierre Hermé has a number of stylish boutiques in Paris in his distinctive colours; the main ones remain at rue Bonaparte in Saint-Germain–des-Prés near the église Saint-Sulpice, and out in the *petit-bourgeois* 15th arrondissement on the lengthy rue de Vaugirard.

Cupcakes

～

*M*uch to the astonishment of the pâtisserie old school, cupcakes are selling like *gâteaux chaud* in the French capital. Shops selling these distinctly non-French, fancy-pants fripperies have been popping up all over Paris. The global fashion for these mega-sweet, outrageously decorated, paper-cased novelties arrived in Paris a few years back and triggered a feeding frenzy of followers all in search of a crazy calorific sugar fix.

With their flashy flamboyance and full-on frosting, I'm guessing the birthplace of the cupcake – sometimes called a fairy cake in Britain – is the USA. Although their beginnings are not well documented, there is a mention of a cake baked in small cups in *American Cookery*, a cookbook by Amelia Simms written in 1796; but the term 'cupcake' was probably first coined in 1828 in American writer Eliza Leslie's *Seventy-five Receipts for Pastry, Cakes, and Sweetmeats*. Similar recipes appear in various British recipe books around the same time.

At the weekend, on the rue Rambuteau, long queues of sugar-obsessed Parisians form outside Berko Bakery, an American-style bakery with a French spin (or maybe it's the other way round) selling loopy-coloured crimson-red, hot-pink and fluorescent-green cupcakes often adorned with popular American candies – they even do one created with Oreo cookies. Cheesecakes are a speciality, too, made with the proper Philadelphia cream cheese and a graham cracker (similar to a digestive biscuit) base, the way the folks like 'em back home.

Across the river, the beautifully choreographed window displays of Synie's Cupcakes showcase her irresistible and highly original creations. With flavours that just dance on the tongue, such as lemon ginger and *dulce de leche* with sea salt or lavender cupcakes with edible flowers, her savoury cupcakes are even more adventurous. Maybe you fancy a cupcake with caramelised onions and cheese on top, or red pepper and pine nuts, perhaps even sesame with herbs and *fromage blanc*? Here is a cupcake creator blissfully pushing the envelope, or more correctly the paper case, as they say in *The Right Stuff*.

Up on the risqué Pigalle hill, a new pouting-pink *petits gâteaux* parlour-cum-cupcakerie has opened called Chloé.S. It's owned by the cupcake princess of the same name, whose pizzazz and passion for all things pink make it a fitting tribute to the crazy kitsch rock 'n' roll cupcake culture that would make Betty Crocker blush in her grave. One of Chloé's more coquettish cupcakes, the '*Florane*', combines chocolate, pear and honey and is topped with a rich, caramel butter cream. Or try the aptly named 'Betty' chocolate cupcake made with peanut butter and capped with a peanut butter cream.

The craze for cupcakes continues unabated in this sybaritic city of sweet pleasure-seekers. Much to the astonishment of the patisserie old school, these distinctly non-French mounds of fun, have been invading traditional pâtisseries and glaciers, and have even been spotted in the supermarket Monoprix.

Mon Dieu – is nothing sacred?

CHOCOLATE CUPCAKES WITH ROSE MARSHMALLOW TOPPING

As both brownies and marshmallows are the happening thing in Paris, these cupcakes just had to make their debut in this book. I'm not a big fan of the boring sponge base used in many cupcake recipes or, for that matter, of heaps of over-sweet frosting that tastes only of sugar. So a brownie base with a more subtle, rose-scented marshmallow topping makes a more sophisticated alternative. You can buy rose syrup online or from select fine food stores. For decoration I've opted for simple sugared rose petals but you don't have to hold back — the world is your cupcake!

. . . .

MAKES 12

FOR THE BASE
60 g (2¼oz) bittersweet dark chocolate
60 g (2¼ oz) unsalted butter, diced
60 g (2¼ oz) caster (superfine) sugar
1 egg
35 g (1¼ oz) plain (all-purpose) flour, sifted
1½ tablespoons cocoa powder
¼ teaspoon baking powder

FOR THE TOPPING
200 g (7 oz) caster (superfine) sugar
250 ml (9 fl oz/1 cup) water
1 tablespoon glucose syrup
1 teaspoon gelatine powder
2 large egg whites
3 teaspoons rose syrup

Sugared rose petals, to decorate

Preheat the oven to 160°C/325°F/gas mark 3 and line a 12-hole muffin tin with paper cases.

Over a low heat, melt the chocolate and butter in a saucepan, stirring until smooth.

While this is cooling mix the sugar, egg, flour, cocoa powder and baking powder in a separate bowl, then combine with the chocolate mixture until smooth.

Spoon into the paper cases, filling only about halfway, and bake for 10–12 minutes until cooked. Leave to cool completely.

To make the marshmallow topping, heat the sugar, water, glucose syrup and gelatine powder in a small saucepan, stirring gently. Bring to the boil and simmer for about 5 minutes, then leave to cool slightly.

Beat the egg whites until stiff, preferably with an electric whisk, and continue to whisk while folding in the still hot sugar syrup until the mixture becomes shiny and starts to thicken. Add the rose syrup and continue whisking for 5–10 minutes, until the mixture is stiff and thick enough to hold its shape on the whisk.

Pipe or spoon the marshmallow over the top of the brownie bases and refrigerate until set. Decorate with sugared rose petals – or go to town!

Meringues and Brownies

~

Meringues – a stalwart among pastry-makers – have recently enjoyed a renaissance in Paris. Once the quintessential Sunday dessert in France, served with a centre filling of *crème Chantilly*, over time meringues became less popular although they remain an essential constituent of the *Mont Blanc* and other pastries.

The origin of the name 'meringue' is a bit of a mystery. Some claim it comes from the town of Möhringen in the defunct duchy of Saxe-Coburg; others that it hails from Meiringen, a municipality in the canton of Bern, Switzerland. The story goes that in the early eighteenth century a Swiss pastry chef called Casparini decided to use up some leftover egg whites, so he whipped them with powdered sugar and popped them in the oven. The result was a fluffy, light, sugary confection. The current spelling of meringue appeared in François Massialot's cookbook, *'Nouveau Cuisinier Royal et Bourgeois'* (1691). But if you think all of this is a lot of hot air you could be right; in the Loire region, slow-baked meringues are still referred to as 'pets', meaning farts – presumably due to their light, fluffy texture!

In the nineteenth century, the father of *haute cuisine*, Antonin Carême, pioneered the use of a pastry bag with a fluted tip, giving birth to the ridged, peaked floral appearance that is found in French pâtisseries today. Until then, meringues had been shaped between two large spoons. For years you would see a puffy pile of these craggy mountains of sugary egg white in the window of nearly every respectable French pastry shop and bakery. I had always assumed they were bought for making desserts at home and not for eating on their own. But this is all changing. Au Merveilleux de Fred – named after M Frédéric Vaucamp, who trained at the legendary Lenôtre before opening his first meringue shop in Lille and then rolling out to the capital – is among a number of whimsical boutiques scattered around Paris dedicated to a modern-style meringue. With irresistible names like *'Le Merveilleux'*, *'L'Incroyable'* and *'L'Impensable'*, these are meringues not as we know them…

Big, fat, fudgy, funky, choco-loaded brownies are about as American as apple pie. Along with other imports like cupcakes, cheeseburgers and Ralph Lauren, the *brownie au chocolat* has become almost as popular with Parisians as freshly baked baguettes. Championed by the American-style bakeries and eateries that have gained a firm foothold with expats and Parisians alike, the brownie is getting an equally big showing in the traditional pâtisseries, boulangeries and tea salons.

In Paris these ubiquitous squares of intense cocoa flavour are almost invariably made with dark chocolate and often include nuts, milk and white chocolate, pistachios or banana – even milk chocolate brownies are not unheard of. For those homeboys nostalgic for this home-grown goodie, there is the American-styled Bagels & Brownies in Montparnasse or, up in the 8th, the excellent Japanese pâtisserie, La Petit Rose. Brownies don't come better than here!

MERINGUES MODERNES

I know it's a bit of a cheek but I believe this recipe is an improvement on the more traditional technique for French meringues employed by patisseries all over Paris. As a rule, they only use egg white and icing sugar, which I find a bit too brittle and powdery, and they often explode into shards when you try to eat them. Coming from a country where perfect meringue-making is a rite of passage, I have felt compelled to try to improve on a French classic. Forgive my audacity, but I think this meringue has a more delicate texture and will just melt in the mouth, and you end up with soft, gooey, marshmallow-like centres.

MAKES 12

4 egg whites
120 g (4¼ oz/½ cup) caster
   (superfine) sugar
½ teaspoon vanilla extract
1 teaspoon white wine
   vinegar
110 g (3¾ oz) icing
   (confectioner's) sugar

FOR THE FILLING
150 g (5½ oz) fresh
   raspberries
2 teaspoons caster
   (superfine) sugar
125 g (4½ oz) white
   chocolate
60 ml (2 fl oz) double (heavy)
   cream

Preheat the oven to 150°C/300°F/gas mark 2, and lightly oil and line a large baking sheet with baking paper and lightly smear this too.

Using an electric whisk, beat the egg whites to stiff peaks. Don't try this with a hand whisk – it won't work. Continue to whisk, folding in the caster sugar about 1 tablespoon at a time and waiting until it is completely incorporated before adding another. To tell if the sugar has dissolved, rub a bit of the mixture between your fingers. If it feels gritty, the sugar hasn't dissolved, so keep beating for a few minutes. Then add the vanilla extract and vinegar. It should take at least 10 minutes for the mixture to become smooth and glossy.

Gradually fold in the icing sugar with a spatula until fully incorporated. Spoon out in 24 large dollops on the baking sheet, using the back of the spoon to create swirls. Allow at least 5 cm (2 inches) between each meringue.

Reduce the oven to 140°C/275°F/gas mark 1 and bake on the middle shelf for 45 minutes, then turn off the oven, open the door and leave to gently cool on the oven shelf for 15 minutes, for gooey centres.

For the raspberry white chocolate filling, first make a raspberry purée. Place the raspberries in a pan with the sugar and heat gently until the sugar dissolves, the raspberries release their juice and the purée is concentrated. Strain through a fine sieve and put aside to cool.

Finely chop the chocolate with a knife and place in a heatproof mixing bowl. Heat the cream in a medium saucepan and bring almost to the boil, then pour over the chocolate and combine in a circular movement until the mixture is smooth, and then add 2 tablespoons of the raspberry purée.

Leave to cool but don't refrigerate. When cool, spoon onto the inside of one meringue and then sandwich together with another. Continue until all the meringues have been used up. Store in an airtight container for up to 5 days.

FRENCH-STYLE CHOCOLATE-CHIP BROWNIES

These to-die-for brownies are very much a Parisian chocolatier's take on what is now a peripatetic American declaration of deliciousness. It's a mega-rich, decadent, fudgy type of brownie loaded with large chunks of white and milk chocolate. You can also add pecan, hazel or walnuts if that's your thing.

....

MAKES ABOUT 16 SQUARES

185 g (6½ oz) unsalted butter, diced, plus extra for greasing
2 vanilla pods
180 g (6⅓ oz) bittersweet dark chocolate
2 large eggs
2 egg yolks
250 g (9oz) golden caster (superfine) sugar
150 g (5½ oz/1 cup) plain (all-purpose) flour
50 g (1¾ oz) cocoa powder
75 g (2¾ oz) white chocolate, chopped
75 g (2¾ oz) milk chocolate, chopped

Preheat the oven to 180°C/350°F/gas mark 4 and grease a 23 x 23 cm (9 x 9 inches) square baking tin.

Using a sharp knife, split the vanilla pods lengthways and scrape out the seeds. Set aside.

Chop the dark chocolate into small pieces and melt with the diced butter in a heatproof bowl over a saucepan of simmering water. Allow to cool slightly.

Using an electric mixer, beat the eggs, egg yolks, sugar and vanilla seeds together in a separate bowl until smooth and creamy. Add the chocolate and butter mixture and whisk until combined. Then sift the flour and cocoa powder together and, with a wooden spoon, fold into the mixture. Finally, use a spatula to stir in the white and milk chocolate chunks.

Pour into the greased tin and bake for 20–25 minutes, or until the brownie is just pulling away from the sides; the centre should still be moist but not runny. Allow to cool then cut into squares.

Guimauve

~

One of the things the French love to remember most are the nostalgic sweets from their childhood. And nothing is more evocative of this wistful wander down memory lane than *guimauve*, or marshmallow, a candy so historic it can be traced back to ancient Egypt. Although it bears little resemblance to its saccharine, spongy, pastel, puffed up, pinky, cotton-wool-tasting American cousin, it is made from the same ingredients but, quite naturally, with a lot of French flair. More recently, this much-loved confection of yesteryear has made a comeback and is now at risk of gaining a cult following. Strange as it might seem, the Parisians are going crazy for *guimauve* in its new incarnation. I can't quite put my finger on why but I think it is largely down to its patronage by a number of fashionable pâtisseries and confiseries, which have embraced the trend for the marshmallow nouveau.

American visitors and boy scouts alike may well have trouble recognising the French version of the cylindrical shaped thing they toast over a campfire while singing *Ging Gang Goolie* or other such gibberish; they will also discover there is more than a slight price discrepancy. The French make theirs in a rustic, homemade style in all shapes and sizes, from more conformist cubes to long rectangular strips that resemble something you might use to stop draughts under doors. They even tie them in knots. The colours give some clue as to the flavours. Ranging from the conventional pink and white, they go on to cover a rainbow spectrum: bright pistachio greens, deep purple, dirty chocolatey browns and fluorescent orange are all on the colour palette.

Allegedly, Boulangerie Piccadis, a progressive neighbourhood baker in the charmingly named rue Gay Lussac near the Luxembourg gardens, were the first to get things going with this new-style *guimauve* and for all I know that is a fact. They certainly set great store by claiming as such in their shop window. And their *guimauve* is good, damn good. But I guess the hero of the piece is Pain de Sucre. Being in the hip Marais, they are more attuned to the zeitgeist and have made *guimauve* their calling card. Their window sports big glass jars of the block-like stuff: *matcha* green tea, cassis, dark chocolate coated in coconut, angelica and, surprise on top of surprise, saffron and chilli pepper, as well as chicory and whisky. And before you start thinking that the chef has been on that very same whisky bottle, let me reassure you they taste shockingly delicious.

You can now find this French-style marshmallow all over Paris, from Gérard Mulot, À la Mère de Famille, Le Bonbon au Palais and Blé Sucré.

3

Patisserie and Salon de Thé Classics

···

Many of the time-honoured classic pastries, cakes and tarts that we eye up in the windows of the Paris pâtisseries owe their current revival to the skills of Gaston Lenôtre, who in the 1970s revolutionised French pastry-making. Refining the techniques, and ridding them of their unnecessarily intricate sugar-spun embellishments, he also lightened their load by reducing their cream, butter and sugar content. Many famous pastry chefs, such as Pierre Hermé, have followed in his footsteps, adding their own contemporary touches and a sprinkling of magic while reinterpreting these illustrious classics. When we eagerly tuck into an impeccably crafted pastry, it's easy to forget all the skill that has gone into such perfection, the result of years of training by a professional pastry chef who has learnt to use these techniques with scientific precision, providing a feast for our eyes and palate. Whatever your preference, be it an *éclair*, *baba au rhum*, *millefeuille*, *L'Opéra* or *St Honoré*, these enduring masterpieces have become institutions in Paris, rooted in daily ritual; indispensable comforts in a world where a little self-indulgence is essential to a life lived well.

All of us have our favourite pastry or tart. I am passionate about *millefeuilles*, whereas my partner Kumiko would murder for a *Mont Blanc*. Yet how many times have we wanted to try something different, but been put off because we don't know the name? I remember, many years ago, asking the severe-looking madame behind the counter of a particularly high temple Paris pâtisserie for 'that *Saint Honoré* in the window, please'. It was in fact a *religieuse* and she looked at me as though I had suggested taking her daughter for a dirty weekend in Deauville! When I pointed to the pastry I wanted, politely apologising that I might have got the name wrong, she compounded my humiliation with that characteristic weary Gallic shrug and glance to heaven that the French reserve for foreigners.

Fortunately, these incidents are rare today. The modern-day *pâtissier* is altogether more warm and welcoming. Legendary names like Gérard Mulot, Claire Damon from Des Gâteaux et du Pain, Fabrice Le Bourdat from Blé Sucré, Philippe Conticini at La Pâtisserie des Rêves, Christophe Michalak at the Plaza Athénée and many more master chefs are regularly found front of house, making helpful suggestions and charming their customers with their knowledge and passion for their exacting art. This, then, is a somewhat simplified description of the pastries you will find in their hallowed portals, classics that have become part of everyday life in Paris. Selfishly, I have only included my favourites but I hope that you will be persuaded to enter a Parisian pâtisserie with new-found confidence to taste something very special.

~

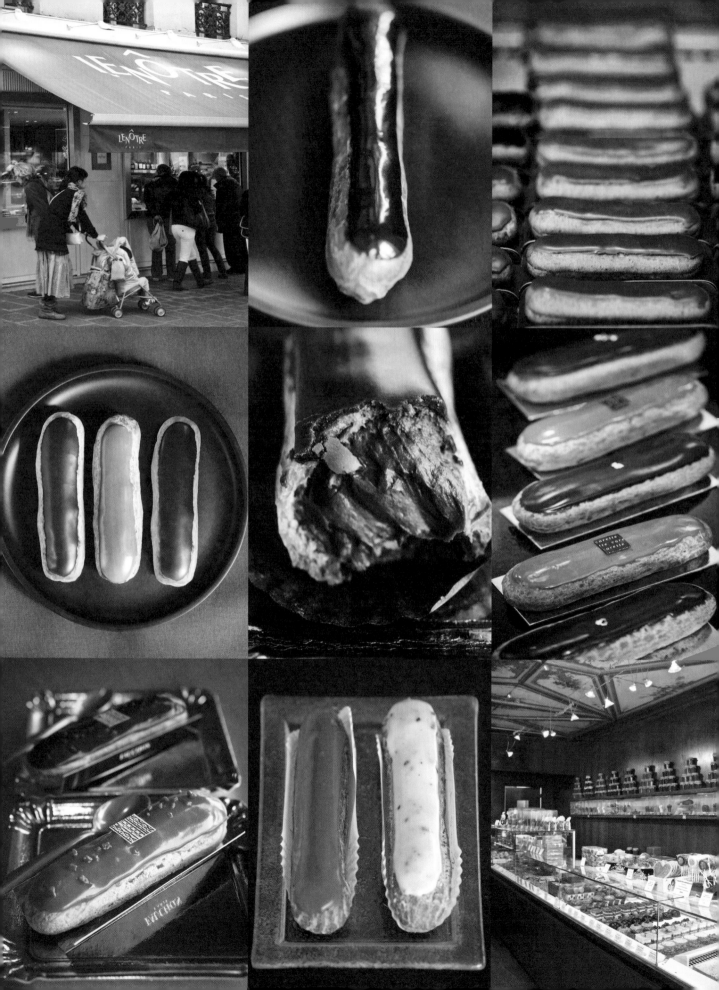

The Éclair

～

Of all the sweet temptations on offer in Paris the enduring chocolate éclair holds pride of place. Dubbed Paris's most popular pastry, you could be forgiven for thinking that most Parisians have a serious choux fetish. No doubt its popularity is due to an ability to deliver a rapid sugar rush and instant oral gratification. Simple, unfussy and a seriously sensuous treat at a very reasonable price, éclairs are the ultimate sweet fast food.

I confess to having a rather major éclair habit myself. Although *aficionados* might disagree, the best éclairs are a combination of a bit of rough with lots of smooth — you want lots of silky-textured chocolate cream complemented by a slightly crisp pastry case. The shell itself is made from choux pastry, or *pâte à choux*, which has to be fresh, airy, soft to the bite and not too doughy. Then comes the *pièce de résistance*: the filling — a combination of divine *crème pâtissière* and rich chocolate. Thick, velvety, creamy and luscious, it shouldn't be too rich or too sweet. Here perfection treads a fine line. Now we come to the shiny, dark chocolate fondant glaze or icing. I like this coating to be a tad on the sharp side, so that it opposes the sweeter, creamy interior. Finally, and this might well upset the purists, I like my éclair to be just slightly chilled, so you get those delicate beads of condensation on top of the glaze.

Of course the ubiquitous éclair isn't restricted to chocolate: caramel, coffee and mocha are just as popular. While purists shun innovation and believe that, skilfully made, the chocolate éclair is perfection itself, the more open-minded éclair acolytes, with a penchant for the wacky, flock to Fauchon for their pop-art creations: a fine layer of white chocolate glaze is printed with a leopard skin motif while Mona Lisa's eyes appear on a milk chocolate version. Over the river, Japanese pastry chef Sadaharu Aoki has turned the éclair into high art with his green tea and sesame seed versions, while Pain de Sucre in the Marais district produce a pineapple éclair and other multi-coloured fruit variants.

The flagging *flâneur* in search of a sweet hit can't really go past the more traditional chocolate éclair, the benchmark by which all good Parisian *pâtissiers* are judged, and Le Figaro magazine frequently hands out accolades for the best éclairs in Paris. Carette, Jean-Paul Hévin, Stohrer, Vandermeersh, La Maison du Chocolat and Ladurée regularly share the top five places. It's hard to challenge this, especially with the likes of Stohrer who have been tempting passers-by on the rue Montorgueil market since 1725. However, I do have a soft spot for Blé Sucré in the 12th. One of my other all-time favourites is Gérard Mulot in Saint-Germain-des-Prés. And of course Jacques Genin, given his dedication to perfection in all that he does, is a difficult éclair to pass up when ambling in the Haut Marais.

CLASSIC FRENCH CHOCOLATE ÉCLAIRS

You may think that a chocolate éclair is much too much trouble to make, but you're wrong. They may be a labour of love, but these delectable chocolate éclairs are well worth the time they take. With a bit of practice, you can soon get your pâte à choux *on the money. Start by baking the éclair cases at a high temperature, and then finish them at a low temperature. The reason for this is that choux pastry is leavened with steam, rather than with baking powder or yeast. The initial high temperature generates the steam which causes it to rise.*

MAKES 10

FOR THE CHOUX PASTRY
65 ml (2¼ fl oz) water
65 ml (2¼ fl oz) whole milk
55 g (2 oz) unsalted butter,
*   at room temperature*
1 tablespoon caster
*   (superfine) sugar*
pinch of fine sea salt
100 g (3½ oz) plain
*   (all-purpose) flour, sieved*
4 eggs, at room temperature

FOR THE FILLING
500 ml (18 fl oz) crème
*   pâtissière, at room*
*   temperature*
*   (see page 74)*
30 g (1 oz) bittersweet dark
*   chocolate*
15 g (½ oz) unsweetened
*   cocoa powder*

FOR THE GLAZE
150 g (5½ oz) bittersweet
*   dark chocolate*
60 g (2¼ oz) unsalted butter
50 g (1¾ oz) icing
*   (confectioner's) sugar*
60 ml (2 fl oz) water

Preheat the oven to 180°C/350°F/gas mark 4 and line a large baking sheet with baking paper. To make the *pâte à choux*, put the water, milk, butter, sugar and salt into a saucepan and bring to the boil. Take off the heat and slowly fold in the flour, stirring with a wooden spoon until smooth.

Return to a medium heat and stir with a wooden spoon for about 2 minutes until the dough comes away from the sides of the pan. Remove from the heat and whisk in the eggs, beaten, one at a time until you have a smooth, dropping consistency. Spoon the mixture into a large piping bag fitted with a 1.5 cm (½ inch) plain nozzle and leave for 5 minutes or so to cool and stiffen slightly.

Pipe 10 large, sausage-shaped éclair shells about 15 cm (6 inches) long on to the baking sheet, spacing them 5 cm (2 inches) apart to allow room to expand. Bake in the oven for 25–30 minutes until golden brown, then transfer to a wire rack and leave to cool. Do not open the oven door during baking, or they will collapse.

To make the filling, have the *crème pâtissière* ready in a bowl. Melt the chocolate in a separate heatproof bowl over a pan of simmering water until there are no lumps. Pour the melted chocolate into the *crème pâtissière*, spoon in the cocoa powder and whisk until smooth, then leave to cool completely.

Transfer the filling to a piping bag fitted with a 5 mm (⅕ inch) nozzle. Using the tip of the nozzle, pierce the underside of the éclairs in three places along the length and gently squeeze in the filling as evenly as possible.

For the glaze, melt the chocolate in the same way as above. When melted, add the butter and sugar, whisking continuously until it looks shiny and creamy. Remove from the heat, leave to cool for 10 minutes, then dip each éclair in the icing and smooth over using a spatula. Wait until the icing hardens before serving.

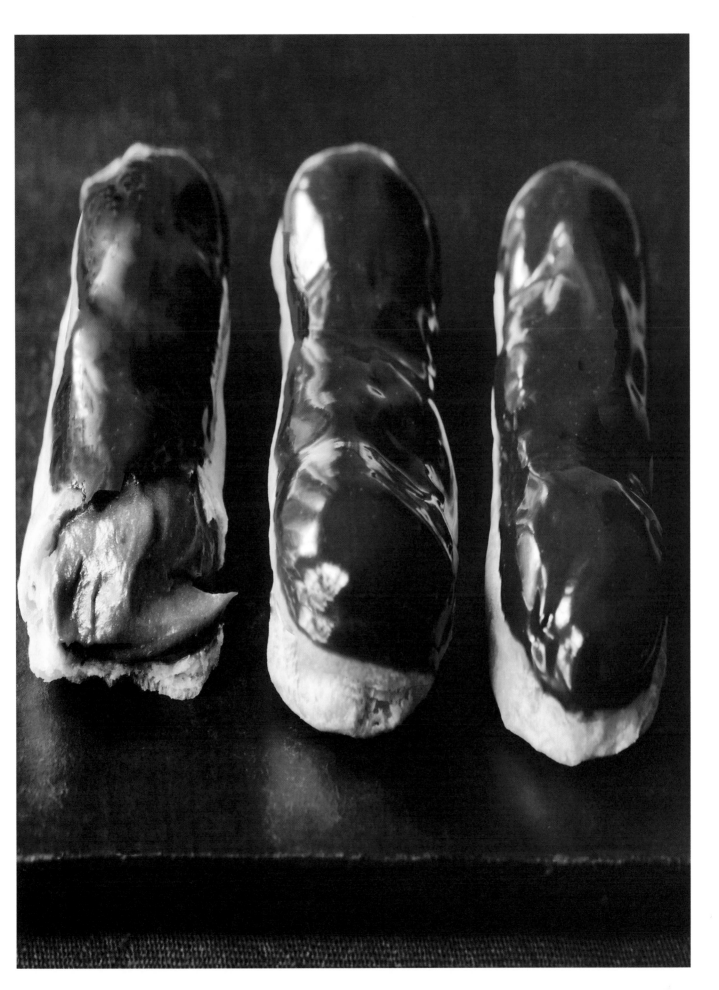

Millefeuilles

⁓

The characteristic multi-layered French *millefeuille*, meaning a 'thousand leaves', is a class act and a firm favourite of mine. Despite the fact that the best *millefeuilles* are to be found in Paris, I have wolfed them down all over the world. Outside of France, they masquerade with potential gangsta rap names like vanilla slice, cream slice and custard slice. In the USA they are known as the 'Napoleon'. Understandably not everyone can pronounce *millefeuille*. Although, to confuse matters more, in France a *Napoleon* is a *millefeuille* filled with almond-flavoured paste.

The origins of the *millefeuille* have become foggy with time. Back in the seventeenth century, that early star of French cuisine, François Pierre de la Varenne, described it as a *'gâteau de mille-feuilles'* in his groundbreaking book *'Le Cuisinier François'*. But it wasn't until the early nineteenth century that the first celebrity chef, Marie-Antoine Carême, known as the 'Chef of Kings', gave the *millefeuille* another mention. Yet it seems the real champion was the Seugnot Pâtisserie in the rue du Bac, in the 7th arrondissement; they 'proposed it for the first time to their customers' in 1867. Monsieur Dubose, the master confectioner of Seugnot, crowned himself the 'King of *Millefeuille*', though he can't have had much competition for the title at the time.

A well-made *millefeuille* is a challenge to eat. I defy anyone not to end up covered in flakes of pastry and *crème pâtissière*, but it is more than worth the inconvenience. As a rule, the classic *millefeuille* is made up of a fragile structure consisting of three layers of *pâte feuilletée*, or puff pastry, which should be as 'light as leaves'. These are interspersed with opulent layers of vanilla-flavoured *crème pâtissière*. Sometimes whipped cream can be substituted but to me this is an abomination. The top is usually glazed with a white fondant icing that is sometimes decorated with a piped marbling effect known as *marbrage*. There are many variations on the basic *millefeuille* theme but here we are interested only in the classic that enshrines the art of fine French pastry skills all over Paris.

There is a plethora of well-regarded pâtisseries in Paris purveying the perfect *millefeuille*, so if I miss out the odd one I hope I will be forgiven. In the east of the city, on the avenue Daumensil, the legendary local baker Vandermeersch comes high on the list, although it maybe a little off the beaten track for some. Jacques Genin, in the Haut Marais, is another of my favourites. His salted butter caramel *millefeuille* is sensational. And Gérard Mulot, my pastry hero on the Left Bank, does an amazing *millefeuille* with berries. From Mulot in the 6th it's a short hop to rue du Bac in the 7th, where Philippe Conticini's contemporary La Pâtisserie des Rêves wows his fans with the sexiest looking *millefeuille* in town. Then, of course, in the rue de Rivoli there is Angelina: their *millefeuille* is as glam as it gets.

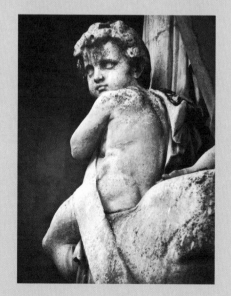

L' Opéra

〜

For this classic, elaborately layered gâteau we have to thank Monsieur Louis Clichy, who premiered it with the rather unoriginal name *'Le Clichy'* at the *Exposition Culinaire* in Paris in 1903. Many years later, the progressive Parisian pâtisserie, Dalloyau, reintroduced and popularised it as *'L'Opéra'*, named after the Paris Grand Opéra – an altogether more fitting title given that it strikes the right note between the nutty sweet chocolate and bitter coffee flavours. Timeless, glamorous, elegant, stylish… *L'Opéra* is the ready-to-eat *haute couture* of *haute cuisine* – the Chanel suit of sweet confections.

A moist, dense chocolate cake, *the gâteau de l'Opéra* is a masterpiece of pâtisserie engineering that can intimidate even the experienced *pâtissier*. Needless to say, it takes an unrivalled talent to successfully construct this subtle symbiosis of complex flavours and texture. It is usually made of seven or eight thin layers, three of which are the delicate almond sponge known as *joconde*, soaked in coffee-rum syrup. This is then interspersed with two more layers of silky coffee butter cream and a single layer of rich, bittersweet chocolate ganache. Finally, these are topped with a thick, luscious layer of dark chocolate glaze. To remove any doubt about what you're eating, it's not unusual for the word *'Opéra'* to be boldly piped or 'stamped' in chocolate across the top, or for individual slices to be garnished with a triumphant chocolate treble clef or flashy flakes of gold leaf.

Traditionally it is served in long, thin rectangular slices, rather than in squares, and due to its richness, it is best consumed with a good cup of black coffee or a fine Armagnac or Cognac. Like the chocolate éclair, I prefer mine slightly chilled but *aficionados* may argue that it should be eaten at room temperature. At any rate, for me the decadent *L'Opéra* really rocks when it's a bit on the cold side.

How do you discover the best in town? *Ce n'est pas un problème.* *L'Opéra* has become an iconic cake in most *salons de thé* and reputable pâtisseries from one end of Paris to the other. Lenôtre is always a good starting point, but despite my deep reverence for its founder I often feel a bit intimidated in these high temples to *haute cuisine*. They are also a little out of my price range. Given its role in championing this cake, Dalloyau should be high on your list. They have a number of shops in Paris. My favourite *gâteau de l'Opéra*, however, can be found at Jean Millet in the 7th and Gérard Mulot in Saint-Germain-des-Prés. Both have achieved perfection. Near the Jardin du Luxembourg, Japanese *pâtissier* Sadaharu Aoki is a close runner-up, and the pâtisserie counter at the Grande Épicerie in the famous Bon Marché department store won't disappoint.

Baba au Rhum

～

Fable has it that the original *baba au rhum*, or rum baba, was introduced into France in the eighteenth century by Stanislaw Leszcynski, the king of Poland who was exiled in Alsace-Lorraine. The legendary Nicolas Stohrer, one of his apprentice *pâtissiers*, developed the basic Polish *babka* – a tall, cylindrical yeast cake – by adding Malaga wine, saffron, raisins and *crème pâtissière*. Implausible as it sounds, it is said that good King Stanislaw was reading *1001 Arabian Nights* at the time and so baptised this new cake the 'Ali Baba'. In 1725 jammy old Nicolas Stohrer became the *maitre pâtissier* to Stanislaw's daughter Maria, following her to the palace of Versailles when she married Louis XV. A few years later, in 1730, escaping the fun and games at Versailles he founded his own pâtisserie in Paris in the rue Montorgueil where it still stands today.

But it wasn't until 1835 that one of M Stohrer's descendants added rum, rather than wine, to a freshly baked brioche-style cake straight out of the mould (the recipe has subsequently been refined by mixing the rum with a bit of sugar syrup). Similar to brioche, the basic batter for a good *baba au rhum* is even richer, using eggs, milk, sugar, butter and, of course, yeast. When cooked, it is soaked in rum, and often filled with whipped cream and *crème pâtissière*. It is usually baked in individual, slightly tapered cylinder moulds but can sometimes be made in a larger size. More developments took place in 1844 when the Julien Brothers came up with the 'Savarin', which was shamelessly inspired by the *baba au rhum*. Soaked in kirsch syrup and used a ring cake mould instead of the simple cylindrical one, to this day there's still a lot of crossover and confusion.

For pundits, Maison Stohrer, at their original shop in the Montorgueil market, still make a *baba au rhum* of the highest order in four varieties: *L'Ali Baba* (the original flavoured with saffron, soaked in rum and topped with *crème pâtissière* and raisins), *Le Baba Chantilly* (garnished with Chantilly cream), *Le Baba rhum nature* (with normal rum) and *Le Baba aux fruits* (topped with berries). But my passion is for the *baba au rhum* created by Pain de Sucre in the Marais, which they dub the 'Baobob'. This reinterpretation of the classic is testament to their inventiveness. A plastic pipette which is stuck in the top of their syrupy cake and filled with a rum-vanilla punch allows you to add the amount of alcohol that suits your mood. The other front-runner in the *baba au rhum* league has to be Blé Sucré, out in the 12th arrondissement near the Marché d'Aligre. The charming Fabrice Le Bourdat makes an exceptional *baba au rhum* that comes with lashings of whipped cream and a thin stick of chocolate. Lastly, for those with deep pockets, Alain Ducasse promotes the *baba au rhum* as his signature dessert in his Michelin-starred restaurant at the Plaza Athénée.

PAIN DE SUCRE

St Honoré and Paris-Brest

~

Over the years, choux pastry, that bedrock of the Parisian pâtisserie, has provided no end of inspiration, as well as challenges, to the city's great pastry chefs. Two of the most popular progeny from their diligence are the much-fêted *St Honoré* and the *Paris-Brest*. The *St Honoré* is named after the French patron saint of pastry chefs, St Honoré or Honoratus, bishop of Amiens in about AD 600, who was credited with a miracle or two in feeding his flock. Fittingly, the memorial church that bears his name is in the fashionable rue Faubourg Saint-Honoré.

This traditional French pastry is still made to the recipe of its nineteenth century creator, the imaginative Monsieur Chiboust. It begins with a puff pastry base crowned with choux pastry balls coated in sticky caramel syrup and filled with *crème chiboust* – a vanilla-based pastry cream with sugar and egg whites added while it's still warm. Finally, the *St Honoré* is held together with lashings of whipped cream, added using a special piping tip and resulting in a glorious togetherness on the plate.

Paris's pastry stars of today have fashioned numerous reworkings of the *St Honoré* theme. Pierre Hermé's delectable *Carrément Chocolat* uses a delicate dark chocolate cream combined with the rich caramelised choux. Or you might be seduced by Ladurée's sensuous rose and raspberry take on this classic. My favourite *St Honoré* can be found at the celebrated Carette (the Place des Vosges *salon de thé* is where I prefer to savour the moment as it's such a stunning location). On the other hand, Fabrice Le Bourdat at Blé Sucré in the 12th makes an equally sumptuous *St Honoré*, as do the skilled pastry chefs at Rollet Pradier in the 7th.

The choux pastry *Paris-Brest* has an equally intriguing past. It was created in 1891 by an enterprising Parisian pastry chef, whose shop was conveniently close to the start of a gruelling long-distance bicycle race from Paris to Brest, a town in Brittany. He made the shrewd decision to commemorate the occasion with a choux pastry cake in the shape of a bicycle wheel. Cut in half and piped with a rich, complex-flavoured hazelnut or praline butter cream and sprinkled with roasted almonds and powdered sugar, it was the undeniable winner of the race. The cake is still created following the traditional recipe but, like all classics, there are also numerous twists on the original.

If a *Paris-Brest* is your thing, rent one of the self-service grey *bicyclettes* found all over Paris and pedal over to Rollet Pradier near the Assemblée Nationale, or take a short spin to Carl Marletti in the 5th to try out their inventive take on this masterpiece of choux construction.

Mont Blanc and Religieuse

~

The *Mont Blanc*, or *Mont-Blanc aux marrons*, is one of the oldest French desserts and dates back to the fifteenth century. Whether it's French or Italian is still in dispute, but the earliest mention is in an Italian cookbook from 1475, which states that the *Mont Blanc* was a favourite in the home of famous femme fatale Lucrezia Borgia. I'd like to think that this indulgent dessert was a blissful distraction from the ruthless Machiavellian politics and sexual corruption alleged characteristic of the Renaissance Papacy, but alas it's just a fantasy.

It is thought the *Mont Blanc* became popular in France in the early part of the seventeenth century. Originally they were yellow, probably as a result of using chestnuts sweetened through a pickling process. But their likeness to a snow-capped mountain no doubt comes from their inner mass of whipped cream and meringue. The present-day configuration was invented by Antoine Rumpelmeyer, an Austrian who founded the landmark tea salon Angelina, back in 1903.

Despite modern pastry-making skills, classic *Mont Blancs* are no works of art compared with more contemporary pastries. In their simplest form, they are made from the finest vanilla-flavoured, sweet, creamy chestnut purée. This is piped in long, vermicelli strands over a mound of *crème Chantilly*, which sits on a base of crumbly meringue. The best *Mont Blancs* are to be found in the autumn when chestnuts are in season, although they're available all year round in many Parisian *salons de thé* and pâtisseries, as they use tinned or frozen purée.

It's no secret that the world-famous Angelina in the rue de Rivoli, patronised by Coco Channel, Marcel Proust and Audrey Hepburn, is as famous for its *Mont Blancs* as it is for its clientele. They claim that over 600 are sold every day from this historic *belle époque* tea-room. Ladurée is another purveyor of the *Mont Blanc*, as are a number of *salons de thé* in Paris. If after queuing to get into these august establishments you have lost the will to live, hotfoot it over to Jean Millet in the 7th, who justifiably ranks among the *Mont Blanc* greats.

The *Religieuse*, a bit like a cream puff derivative of the éclair, is a time-honoured tribute to traditional pastry-making. Contrary to popular belief, it is so-called because of its resemblance to a nun and not because devouring it is the ultimate religious experience. Nevertheless, it takes a leap of faith to see the likeness of mother superior in two profiterole balls of choux pastry filled with a sinfully rich *crème pâtissière*, one on top of the other! The more conventional *religieuses* are covered with either chocolate or coffee icing but there are even prettier, irreverent expressions of this classic, such as Ladurée's highly desirable blackcurrant and violet or rose versions. Blé Sucré make a wickedly delectable *caramel au beurre salé* version, and Carl Marletti has a wonderful pistachio take on the 'nun'. And for the more orthodox style, try the *religieuse* at Carette.

Le Chocolat Chaud

No other Parisian pleasure elicits as many emotive responses as the 'not-so-simple' hot chocolate; and no trip to Paris is complete without a sip or two of this divine concoction.

Chocolate was a big hit in the courts of France when it arrived from the New World in the sixteenth century. In 1657 an inspired chocolatier named David Chaillou opened the first chocolate house in Paris and served a version of hot chocolate mixed with milk. It was an overnight sensation. Marie Antoinette was said to be besotted by this beverage, while some in her court attributed it with aphrodisiac qualities and others believed it to have medicinal benefits.

Partaking of a proper Parisian hot chocolate should be like drinking liquid velvet. The infusion of deep, dark, intense chocolate flavours and spices should produce a sensorial overload on the palate that transports you to paradise. For a genuine hot chocolate in the Parisian method, dispense with the cocoa powder. It's typically made with finely chopped bittersweet chocolate, often from several different sources, melted into hot milk, and sometimes single cream is added. Celebrity chocolatiers jealously guard their recipes, which are enhanced with spices like ginger, chilli and cinnamon and employ exotic cacao sourced from around the globe.

It is widely considered that the mother of all hot chocolates can be found at Angelina, the elegant *belle époque salon de thé* in the rue de Rivoli. Called *'L'Africain'*, it's a thick, dark spicy chocolate served in a single pot with a bowl of whipped cream, usually consumed with a legendary *Mont Blanc* pastry. Jacques Genin, the emperor of chocolate in the Haut Marais, makes a less-sweet *chocolat chaud* using a blend of French chocolates in his laboratory above the shop. For a milder version, the celebrated house of Carette, located either at the Trocadéro or the Place des Vosges, make a delicious Parisian infusion served in classic Limoges china. Another favourite of mine is upstairs at the new chocolate bar at Jean-Paul Hévin in the rue Saint-Honoré. His menu of somewhat whimsical gourmet cocoas designed for different hours of the day may well take your fancy. The two illustrious side-by-side cafés in the Boulevard Saint-Germain, Les Deux Magots and Café Flore, also offer a respectable *chocolat chaud* – but at a price. Further up the boulevard and down a narrow passage you will find Un Dimanche à Paris, the new venture of Pierre Cluizel, where his luxuriant chocolate cocktail is served in a classic rustic pitcher. Finally, at one or two locations of La Maison du Chocolat that have tasting bars they serve some of the richest 'hot choc' in Paris. Their 'Caracas' is not for the faint-hearted, nor is the 'Bacchus', with a shot of dark rum.

OLD-FASHIONED FRENCH CHOCOLAT CHAUD

This authentic French recipe for traditional chocolat chaud à l'ancienne is for those on a mission to discover the ultimate rich hot choccy. If you are one of them, be prepared to have your socks blown off — you'll probably have to loosen your belt, too, as it is thick, creamy, concentrated and utterly indulgent. But, hey, there are times when we just have to let go. Frequent whisking is mandatory, as is the addition of brown sugar and a pinch of sea salt. I go all the way and serve it with whipped cream and, occasionally, a sprinkle of cocoa powder. Extreme hedonists might want to finish with a dash of rum or Kahlua.

SERVES 4

1 vanilla pod
600 ml (20 fl oz) whole milk
250 ml (9fl oz/1 cup) single (pouring) cream
2 tablespoons brown sugar pinch of sea salt
150 g (5½ oz) bittersweet dark chocolate, finely chopped
100 g (3½ oz) milk chocolate, finely chopped
300 ml (10½ fl oz) double (heavy) cream, whipped, to serve

Take the vanilla pod and slit it lengthwise with a small sharp knife. Scrape out the seeds and add them, along with the rest of the pod, to the milk in a large saucepan. Add the cream, brown sugar and a *soupçon* of salt, then warm over a low heat to bring to a simmer, but don't boil.

Take off the heat and fish out the vanilla pod, then add the two types of chopped chocolate, stirring until they melt and the mixture becomes smooth. At this point you need to use a whisk and some elbow power for a couple of minutes until the chocolate is smooth and a little frothy

Reheat again – being careful not to boil – then pour into suitable cups or bowls and serve with whipped cream.

Tarte aux Fraises

~

The delightfully simple, time-honoured strawberry tart still inspires a passionate following. If it's perfect it is close to ecstasy. Best eaten in the summertime when perfumed, succulent French strawberries are at their juiciest, it remains the number one in my league of berry-inspired tarts. It's the smell of the strawberries that does it for me. Even the most composed Parisians can go weak at the knees when encountering the ripe, sweet, luscious red fruit atop a divine, smooth vanilla-scented *crème pâtissière* all encased in a crisp, crumbly delicate pastry. And don't mention a *tarte aux fraises des bois*, or a freshly baked *tartelette aux framboises*, or you will have them salivating like a Parisian poodle.

History has not recorded when, or by whom, this classic combination was created for the first time. Although we will probably never know the identity of the pastry chef responsible for this dazzling culinary contribution, you can be pretty certain that the advancement of the *tarte aux fraises* owes a lot to the skills of men like Chiboust, Gaston Lenôtre and others of their ilk, who perfected *crème pâtissière* and *pâte sucrée*, a light, French pastry crust ideal for sweet tarts.

I am rather partial to pigging out on a *tarte aux fraises* or two while picnicking on the banks of the Seine or the nearest patch of nature. Somehow sunlight always ignites a greater appetite for more risqué recipes. Think of Manet's controversial impressionist painting *Déjeuner sur l'herbe*. I can recall one memorable spring morning sitting in a green deck chair under a flowering cherry tree in the Jardin des Tuileries where, in the interests of market research, I sampled three *tartlettes aux fraises*, each bought at a different pâtisserie. It's a tough job but someone has to do it!

So where are the best strawberry tarts to be found on the streets of Paris? Again, in the past, *Figaro* magazine have done their bit and ranked those scoring highest in a survey entitled *'Le test des meilleures tartes aux fraises de Paris'* – no doubt a worthy piece of work. Gérard Mulot, Jacques Genin and Dalloyau came one, two, three. Certainly I would not dispute these findings, especially in the case of Gérard Mulot, whose square strawberry tarts rank high in my pick of the crop. For my taste, however, the best in show should go to Claire Damon at Des Gâteaux et du Pain, in the far-flung 15th. But Jean Millet in the 7th also produces a *tarte extraordinaire*, as does the contemporary pâtisserie Hugo & Victor, near Le Bon Marché on the Boulevard Raspail. Lastly, in your hunt for perfection you should not leave out the landmark pâtisseries of Lenôtre or that famous Paris institution, Carette.

CLASSIC TARTE AUX FRAISES

This succulent and simple strawberry tart is really only worth making in high summer when strawberries are at their peak and have that incredible, evocative ripe smell redolent of childhood picnics. Try using those tasteless, imported out-of-season substitutes and it just isn't the same. Apart from the best ripe strawberries, the other secret ingredient is thick, rich crème pâtissière, which needs to almost set before you place the strawberries on top. You can use the same recipe for a classic French raspberry tart and most other berry tarts that don't require baking.

. . . .

SERVES 6

1 x 23 cm (9 inch) pre-baked rich shortcrust pastry tart case (or see recipe on page 149 to make your own pâte sucrée)
800 g (1 lb 12¼ oz) strawberries, hulled

FOR THE CRÈME PÂTISSIÈRE
1 vanilla pod
350 ml (12 fl oz) whole milk

6 egg yolks
100 g (3½ oz) caster (superfine) sugar
50 ml (1¾ fl oz) double (heavy) cream
30 g (1 oz) plain (all-purpose) flour, sifted
30 g (1 oz) cornflour, sifted

FOR THE GLAZE
150 g (5½ oz) fresh raspberries
2 tablespoons caster (superfine) sugar

whipped cream or Greek yoghurt, to serve

To make the *crème pâtissière*, slit the vanilla pod lengthwise with a small sharp knife and scrape out the seeds. Add them, along with the pod, to the milk in a suitable saucepan. Bring almost to the boil, being careful not to let it burn, then fish out the vanilla pod.

In a large bowl, combine the egg yolks and sugar until creamy. Add the cream, plain flour and cornflour, and whisk well until smooth. Slowly pour the hot milk into this mixture, whisking constantly.

Return the milk mixture to the saucepan and bring almost to the boil once more, whisking all the time to prevent any lumps from forming. Reduce the heat and continue to simmer for about 5 minutes over a very low heat, while continuing to whisk, then pour the mixture into a bowl and cover with cling film to prevent a skin from forming. Set aside to cool.

When the *crème pâtissière* has cooled, pour into the pastry shell and spread evenly with a spatula until it is about three-quarters full. Be careful not to fill to the top. Cover with as many hulled strawberries as possible with their noses in the air.

For the glaze, place the raspberries in a pan with the sugar and heat gently until the sugar dissolves, the raspberries release their juice and the purée is concentrated. Strain through a fine sieve and when nearly cool brush over each strawberry. Leave for an hour or two for the flavours to blend, then serve with whipped cream or thick Greek yoghurt.

Tarte au Citron

~

This is one of those traditional French tarts that sorts out the men from the boys. It looks so simple but its benign appearance conceals an extraordinary complexity of taste and texture. True *tarte au citron* connoisseurs are known to judge a *pâtissier* by this unpretentious pastry. It is a benchmark of the true passion and expertise of a pastry-maker: day after day he must be able to craft the perfect melt-in-the-mouth dessert.

Most likely Mediterranean in origin, versions of this ubiquitous tart can be found in Spain and Italy as well as France, and recipes dating from the 1650s bear a strong resemblance to the tarts of today. Each year in the South of France, Menton holds a *Fête du Citron*, in which the lemon tart features large; and the *tarte au citron* is an integral part of the celebration of Provençal cuisine.

Regardless of its southern heritage, the *tarte au citron* has earned its spurs as a classic contender in nearly every Paris pâtisserie. Striking the right balance is critical: the true *tarte au citron* – or, to be exact, in many cases *tartelette au citron* – should be a glossy circle of gooey, lemony-yellow, wobbly suaveness encased in a crumbly sweet circle of *pâte sablée* (the richest of French shortcrust pastries, typically made with butter, flour or ground almonds, eggs and sugar, and flavoured with vanilla).

Tarte au citron purists are resistant to decoration but personally I am not opposed to a sprinkling of tangy zest. Others have perfected the art of enhancing the citrus flavours by glazing the top with lemon jelly. It looks great but I am not sure whether it's truly necessary. However, about one thing I am adamant: it should be the tartest of tarts. That subtle yet sharp bite of lemon must cut through the sweet, unctuous *crème* to produce an explosive taste sensation on the tongue. As the song goes – 'it don't mean a thing if it ain't got that zing'.

In recent years Carl Marletti, in the 5th, has been credited by *Figaro* with the best *tartelette au citron* in town, and I can vouch for this – but he can't afford to rest on his laurels. These days my heart is out in the 15th with Mme Damon's most tangy lemony tart in Paris from Des Gâteaux et du Pain. The maestro Gérard Mulot is a close runner-up with the perfect balance of lemon *crème* and sweet pastry. Pierre Hermé calls his scrumptious lemony contender 'le tarte citron au citron' – the double hit of a big slice of zest on top gives it its zing. I am also sweet on Jacques Genin's lemon *tartelette* with its sprinkling of lime zest. Finally, with a well-deserved place in the tart hall of fame is the pale yellow creation of Fabrice Le Bourdat at Blé Sucré out in the 12th.

TRADITIONAL TARTE AU CITRON

Nearly every pâtissier *in France has a different recipe for this masterpiece, often a closely guarded secret handed down through the generations. This is my version of this proverbial French family favourite. A sinfully rich recipe, it uses double cream and six egg yolks, which is the secret of its succulence; the lemon juice and zest give it that tangy oomph. It evokes memories of al fresco feasts on summer nights in Provence, sipping sticky Muscat de Beaumes de Venise with the heady smell of lavender on the warm night air.*

....

SERVES 6–8

300 g (10½ oz) ready-made shortcrust pastry – or see recipe on page 149 to make your own pâte sucrée

75 g (2¾ oz) unsalted butter

150 ml (5 fl oz) double (heavy) cream

2 eggs

6 eggs yolks

160 g (5 oz) caster (superfine) sugar

200 ml (7 fl oz) fresh lemon juice

zest of 2 lemons, finely grated

whipped cream, to serve

Preheat the oven to 180°C/350°F/gas mark 4.

Roll out the pastry to about 3 mm (¹/₁₀ inch) thick and line a 24 cm (9½ inch) round, 4 cm (1½ inch) deep tart or quiche dish. Place a sheet of greaseproof paper over the pastry case and fill with baking beans. Bake blind in the oven for about 10–15 minutes, or until the case is lightly golden brown and slightly crisp but not completely cooked.

In a medium-size saucepan, gently melt the butter, then slowly add the cream keeping on a low heat. Once this mixture is thoroughly combined, set it aside.

In a separate heatproof bowl placed over a large pan of simmering water, whisk together the eggs, egg yolks and sugar, continuing until the sugar dissolves. Add the lemon juice, stirring constantly for 3 minutes. Add the lemon zest and then the butter and cream mixture, and continue to simmer, stirring constantly, for 5 minutes.

Lower the oven temperature to 150°C/300°F/gas mark 2. Now pour the lemon filling into the prepared pastry case and bake for 30–35 minutes, until it turns a deep golden yellow and the filling is still just a bit wobbly in the middle. If the top shows signs of browning, lay a sheet of foil over to protect it. Remove from the oven and leave to cool slowly. Serve with whipped cream.

4

Traditional Viennoiserie

....

As most people will know, the generic term in France for Viennese-influenced pastries and breads is *viennoiserie*. It all began in 1839 when an enterprising Austrian artillery officer named August Zang opened the Boulangerie Viennoise at 92, rue de Richelieu. The Viennese specialities on sale, including the *Kipferl* – which because of its shape soon became known as the '*croissant*' – were a big hit with Parisian pastry lovers. These goodies inspired a raft of imitations by covetous French chefs, who added Viennese-style pastries to their daily array. The French writer Alphonse Daudet mentions the term '*pâtisseries viennoises*' in a novel written in 1877, but probably by the late nineteenth century they became known as '*viennoiserie*' – ironic, perhaps, when you consider that the common croissant is the embodiment of all that is French. Other more traditional French products with no Teutonic parentage, such as brioche, also came under the *viennoiserie* heading. Nowadays, it largely encompasses baked 'brown' pastries made from brioche or croissant-style puff pastry which use yeast-leavened doughs – although others, such as the *pain aux raisins*, are leavened by butter. For reasons that completely elude me, *madeleines* and *financiers* fall under this banner too, while some fruit tarts such as *tarte au pommes* also seem to be more at home here.

With this heritage, *viennoiserie* were more traditionally made by bakers, but they were soon produced by Parisian *pâtissiers* who added their own refinements. Today *viennoiserie* pastries are familiar fixtures in just about every boulangerie, pâtisserie, *salon de thé* and supermarket throughout France, commanding their own special section within the store. I suppose most of us associate them with breakfast but of course they're also eaten as snacks at any time of the day. There are also numerous seasonal variants, such as *galette des rois*, which is consumed at New Year.

During early morning strolls through the streets of Paris I have without question consumed my share of these 'carbo-loaded' Viennese temptations. After a night on the tiles, they can be a life-affirming treat! But because they are so widespread, it isn't always easy to track down the best *viennoiserie* available in a city as extensive as Paris. So please forgive me if miss out your favourite neighbourhood baker or croissant-maker. I have largely confined my comments to central, or visitors', Paris. And selfishly I have focused only on the *viennoiserie* that I prefer and are possibly among the more popular in Paris. Delicious as it is, the *Kugelhopf* isn't that widely available so it has been left out, as has the *canelé*, which I hanker after but associate more with Bordeaux. And the *palmier* I find fairly bland so it, too, has been left off the list.

~

Croissants

~

The iconic breakfast croissant is said to owe its popularity in Paris to the ill-fated Marie Antoinette, who was Austrian by birth. It was supposedly invented by a quick-thinking Viennese baker in 1683, who foiled a plot by Ottoman invaders to tunnel into the city. He was rewarded with a stash of flour, left behind by the Turkish tunnellers. As a mark of his appreciation, he baked a buttery bread in the shape of the crescent emblem on the Ottoman flag and it became the foremost pastry in Vienna. When the Archduchess of Austria married Louis XVI, she brought the recipe to France as a memento of her charmed childhood. It's a good story but probably all a pile of far-fetched piffle – or in this case *'Kipferl'*, a cousin of the croissant that was documented in Austria as far back as the thirteenth century.

Notwithstanding the fact that crescent-shaped breads and cakes venerating the moon have been around since the Middle Ages, the French croissant really came into its own in nineteenth-century Paris. The early form of the croissant was popularised by August Zang's Boulangerie Viennoise, and the Viennese *Kipferl*, which morphed into the croissant, soon graced the breakfast tables of the Parisian *haut monde*. Then, in the 1920s, a chef with a penchant for puff pastry transformed the ever-evolving *Kipferl* into the contemporary buttery, flaky croissant that we find irresistible today.

As any baker will tell you, making the perfect croissant is an exercise in origami. It's all in the folding, or 'laminating' as the technique is commonly known. It sounds intimidating but it's actually rather simple. Authentic croissants are made with a leavened alternative of puff pastry, where the yeast-risen dough is layered with butter, rolled and folded several times in succession, cut into a triangle with a croissant cutter, then rolled into a scroll with a bulging centre which is then curved into its familiar signature shape.

Connoisseurs of the perfect croissant demand a crunchy, caramelised exterior (called a *Maillard* reaction) that crackles when you bite into it and, importantly, a soft, honeycombed interior as light as air that smells freshly baked and has a very subtle hint of salt. My own approach is much less sophisticated – I scoff them down with slabs of creamy butter and lashings of a slightly tart, homemade apricot jam from Provence. Almond versions stuffed with nutty paste are a rustic, sweet alternative on this popular puff pastry staple.

Ranking the best croissants in Paris is about as contentious as French politics. Everyone has their own opinion, and there is no end of knowledgeable blogs devoted to the subject that passionately argue their definitive lists. So I am going to fuel the controversy even further and opt for only one or two bakeries that light my fire. Poilâne and Du Pain et des Idées both do excellent croissants, but when it comes to the crunch, for me it's a close-run thing between Blé Sucré in the 12th and Des Gâteaux et du Pain out in the petit–bourgeois 15th. Both achieve perfection.

Brioche

~

This eggy, buttery, puffy half-bread, half-pastry is not Austrian but French in origin. It has many paradoxes: made basically in the same way as leavened bread, it has all the intense qualities of a *viennoiserie* pastry. As with pastry, it is enriched with eggs, butter, sugar, milk and sometimes cream but it has the airy texture of bread. It can also be a cake or a pudding, and sweet or savoury. In its sweet form it is often made with fresh or candied fruit, chocolate, or with coarse grains of sugar on top. In this guise, it is usually considered a pastry and is the basis for a variety of desserts with ingredients, fillings or toppings added. In its savoury form, it can be stuffed with vegetables, meat or cheese, while the dough is rather undiplomatically used for the classic Beef Wellington.

Brioche in its many forms is one of the great French nursery comfort foods that evokes memories of blissful childhoods filled with the fragrant yeasty smell of baking brioche radiating from the kitchen. Yet its past is cloaked in controversy. It gave rise to perhaps the most misattributed phrase in French history: 'Let them eat cake', attributed to the much maligned Marie-Antoinette.

In his autobiography, '*Confessions*', the philosopher Jean-Jacques Rousseau recounts that 'a great princess' is said to have recommended to those peasants who had no bread, '*Qu'ils mangent de la brioche*', which was possibly in response to the lack of 'blessed bread', or *pain bénit*, often distributed to the poor by the Church. The accuracy of the story remains doubtful but most modern historians now agree that Marie Antionette was not the 'great princess' in question. And it is possible that there was no mockery intended and that the unnamed 'great princess' was probably just trying to make some useful dietary suggestions. We will never know!

Brioche had been recorded as far back as the fifteenth century, and was more common in Normandy and the north of France where butter was plentiful. It is believed to have developed from *pain bénit*, which was transformed over time as better quality ingredients were added. By the eighteenth century *pain bénit* was frequently replaced by brioche and served on religious occasions such as Epiphany. Refined by generations of bakers and pastry chefs, it gradually evolved into the brioche recipe that we know today.

The distinctive *brioche parisienne* or *brioche à tête*, with its little topknot and attractive scalloped bottom, is perhaps the most commonly recognised shape. Baked in individual round, flared fluted tins, a ball of dough is stuck in the base and topped with a smaller ball to form the head. Enjoyed with slivers of creamy Charente butter and sweet raspberry conserve, it has become the classic breakfast complement to a steaming cup of *café crème*.

So who gets the vote for the best brioche in town? The runners-up are Pain de Sucre in the Marais and Gérard Mulot on the Left Bank, but the title once again goes to Des Gâteaux et du Pain out in the 15th.

BRIOCHE NANTERRE

Try this flaky, buttery brioche loaf with a fragrant light interior and a glossy tanned exterior. Brioche made in a loaf tin is known as brioche nanterre. *Instead of rolling two balls of dough and baking them in individual tins, two longer rows of dough balls are placed in the tin and allowed to rise (prove) which fuses it all together. The quantity of butter results in a rich, decadent dough that bakes into a deliciously golden brioche. Use a good-quality French unsalted butter for the best results.*

. . . .

SERVES 8

2½ teaspoons dried yeast

2 tablespoons lukewarm
   water

2 tablespoons caster
   (superfine) sugar

250 g (9 oz) strong white
   (bread) flour

½ teaspoon sea salt flakes

4 eggs, lightly beaten

225 g (8 oz) unsalted butter,
   diced, at room temperature

FOR THE GLAZE

1 egg

Sprinkle the yeast into the water in a bowl and leave in a warm place for 5 minutes until bubbles appear.

In a separate bowl, combine the sugar, flour and salt. Pour the flour and the yeast mixture into the bowl of an electric mixer fitted with the dough hook. Mix on a low speed and then add the eggs.

Beat on low for one minute and then increase the speed to high for 10 minutes until the dough comes away from the sides of the bowl. Add the butter gradually and beat for another 5 minutes until glossy and elastic.

Transfer the dough to a large bowl, cover with a tea towel and leave at room temperature for 2 hours until the dough has doubled in size. Lift the sticky risen dough and divide into four equal pieces, then roll each piece into a ball, kneading it until smooth.

Place the four balls closely side by side in a lightly buttered loaf tin approx 23 x 10 cm (9 x 4 inches). Cover again with a damp cloth and leave at room temperature for ½ hour. Preheat the oven to 180°C/350°F/gas mark 4. When ready to bake, using a pair of scissors, cut a cross in each ball before glazing. For the glaze, lightly beat the egg and brush over the top.

Bake for 20–25 minutes until well-risen and golden brown (but be very careful not to overcook), then cool on a wire rack. Serve while still warm with creamy French butter and a homemade conserve.

Pain au Chocolat
and Pain aux Raisins
~

The delicious *pain au chocolat* is a close cousin of the croissant. Known as the *chocolatine* in south-western France and Canada, in some countries they are even called chocolate croissants. Usually sold warm from the oven alongside croissants, the *pain au chocolat* is made using the same puff pastry method – a laminated piece of yeast-leavened dough, but with a slab of chocolate in the centre. These chubby, crunchy rectangles blend the sweetness of the flaky, airy buttery pastry with the bitter sweetness of the smooth chocolate. It's a marriage made in chocolate heaven.

My much-loved mid-morning treat probably didn't get a look in until the mid-nineteenth century when the chocolate bar was invented. History doesn't record who actually made the first *pain au chocolat* but like the brioche its origins are more likely to be French than Viennese. Whoever it was started something big. These days they're one of the most popular after-school treats in France. Who knows how many are wolfed down each day in Paris, let alone the big wide world.

Who does the best *pain au chocolat* in Paris? It's a close-run thing between Des Gâteaux et du Pain and Du Pain et des Idées, who I think get it by a short straw. This award-winning neighbourhood boulangerie near the canal St Martin in the 10th, run by the intrepid Christophe Vasseur, is indeed filled with 'bread and ideas'. Try his delectable *banana pain au chocolat* too – but do get there early.

I have to confess that the *pain aux raisins* is my all-time favourite *viennoiserie*. What could be better than a warm, crisp, sweet brioche dough pastry generously filled with oozing, eggy *crème pâtissière* and stuffed with succulent, rum-soaked juicy raisins, all finished off with a sticky, jammy glaze that when baked completely caramelises the entire pastry? I would swim across the Seine even if it was shark-infested for just one bite of the best *pain aux raisins* in Paris.

Sadly, its spiral shape earns the *pain aux raisins* such inopportune aliases as raisin roll, *escargot*, snail and, I'm sure, other nicknames.

The calorie-loaded pastry base, which uses butter as its leavening agent, makes the *pain aux raisins* an intricate one to make as the butter must be kept at a precise temperature for the flaky pastry to become light and airy. It's also important not to overbake the exterior so it becomes dry and the raisins shrivel up. Happily, there are those *pâtissiers* in Paris that excel at this spiralled indulgence. Blé Sucré gets it spot on as does the historic boulangerie Moulin de la Vierge in the 7th and at other locations around Paris. And, of course, I can't leave out my other two favourites, Des Gâteaux et du Pain in the 15th and Du Pain et des Idées in the 10th.

Madeleines

~

Thanks to novelist Valentin Louis Georges Eugène Marcel Proust, this small, rich, scallop-shaped sponge cake has been forever immortalised in French culture. In his autobiographical novel *In Search of Lost Time* there is a crucial scene in which the *madeleine* enables the protagonist to experience the past completely as a simultaneous part of his present existence. Apart from Marcel putting the *madeleine* on the map, these little cakes remain a fond childhood memory for most French people, who habitually dunk them into their tea. In fact, they are so entrenched in French 'dipping' tradition that they were chosen to represent France in the Café Europe initiative of the European Union on Europe Day 2006.

Like many old-fashioned favourites with nostalgic attachments, romantic fables surround their origins. Contrary to what you might think, they don't seem to be named after St Mary Magdalene or the landmark Paris church. Some sources suggest that they may have been named after Madeleine Paulmier, a nineteenth-century pastry cook, but another conflicting legend relates that they originated in the eighteenth century, in the town of Commercy in Alsace-Lorraine. Apparently, a servant of the deposed king of Poland, Stanisław Leszcynski, first baked them in real scallop shells, a traditional emblem for pilgrims who passed through Commercy on their way to Santiago de Compostela in Spain. The sweet-toothed Stanisław was so enamoured of these soft, lemony butter cakes that he graciously named them after the servant, who, you guessed it, was called Madeleine. Whatever the truth, it does make for a good story.

Perfect *madeleines* are made with the finest French flour and baked with the best butter, ideally from the Charente region which produces the richest, creamiest in France. Made with a *génoise* batter or sponge, which combines butter, sugar, eggs and flour, they are conventionally flavoured with lemon or orange flower water and then topped with a sweet, zingy citrus glaze. This finishing touch is for me the 'icing on the cake' that puts them on that Proustian pedestal for writers to rave about. Pundits agree that these dainty, delicate nibbles should be moist, golden-crusted, zesty and have the scent of bronzed butter. And as a testament to King Stanisław's generous gesture, they are traditionally baked in a distinctive shell-shaped moulded tin to resemble the pilgrims' scallop (see recipe overleaf).

Nearly every good *pâtissier* in Paris produces their version of this popular staple, so tracking down the very best takes some doing. Have no fear, though, Hugo & Victor on the Boulevard Raspail in the 7th make some mean *madeleines* which deserve every accolade they get. But for me Fabrice Le Bourdat, owner of Blé Sucré out in the 12th, takes the biscuit. If Monsieur Proust was alive today, this is surely where he would head.

TRADITIONAL MADELEINES WITH ORANGE GLAZE

The madeleine, *an inseparable part of French childhood, is really easy to make. This recipe comes close to what you will find in the pâtisseries of Paris. It uses orange zest and glaze, but these are optional extras. Many traditional recipes also use lemon. Ideally, you will need a traditional* madeleine *baking tin or mould with shell-shaped depressions, but don't be put off if you don't have one - you can get away with a shallow muffin tin instead. They are best munched the day they're made but can be stored for a few days in an airtight container.*

....

MAKES ABOUT 24

130 g (4¾ oz) unsalted
   butter, ideally Charente,
   plus extra for greasing
3 eggs, at room temperature
1 egg yolk
120 g (4½ oz) granulated
   sugar
pinch of salt
175 g (6 oz) plain
   (all-purpose) flour, plus
   extra for dusting
1 teaspoon baking powder
zest of 2 medium oranges

FOR THE GLAZE
150 g (5½ oz) icing
   (confectioner's) sugar
2 tablespoons freshly
   squeezed orange juice

Melt the butter in a small saucepan on a medium heat until it just starts to turn a golden brown and develops a slightly nutty flavour – but be careful not to overheat. Set aside to cool.

Generously grease a madeleine tin or mould with a little of the melted butter. Dust with flour and place in the fridge.

Using a standing electric mixer, whisk the eggs, egg yolk, sugar and salt for 5 minutes until frothy and the batter starts to thicken.

Sift the flour and baking powder and then use a spatula to fold the flour into the batter mixture.

Add the orange zest to the cooled butter, then slowly drizzle the butter into the batter, stirring the mixture until you have folded in all the butter.

Cover the bowl and pop in the fridge for at least 1½ hours. Preheat the oven to 220°C/425°F/gas mark 7.

Drop the batter in the middle of each mould until about three-quarters full – don't worry if it's not accurate. However, it's best not to spread it. Bake for 8–9 minutes in the upper third of your oven until the tops slightly brown or they feel set to the touch.

To make the glaze, stir together the icing sugar and orange juice until really smooth.

Remove the madeleines from the oven and tip on to a cooling rack. When cool, apply the glaze with a pastry brush, turning them over to make sure both sides are coated. Leave on the rack until the glaze has set.

Financiers

~

The French *financier*, or *friand* as it's called in other parts of the world, is a particular party piece of mine – not because of its fiscal connections but solely because of its delicious simplicity. The name derives from the characteristic rectangular mould in which it is baked, which resembles a bar of gold. So, you'll be relieved to know has nothing to do with its popularity with bankers or with the financial district of Paris.

The *financier* has ambiguous beginnings. It probably originated in one form or another in the Mediterranean region, where almonds were plentiful. Today this light, moist, nutty tea cake, which is not dissimilar to a sponge, is a much-loved Parisian snack. Made from ground almonds, flour, egg whites and icing sugar, the heart of the matter is the *beurre noisette* – a French term for 'brown butter' or, literally, 'hazelnut butter'. In brief, it is the best quality butter heated in a saucepan until it turns a golden brown and develops a nutty flavour. Sometimes crushed almonds are added but I am not in favour of introducing too many bits and bobs or deviating too far from the recipe's honest unfussiness.

Its closest cousin, the antipodean *friand*, which has spread down-under like a rampant bushfire uses the same recipe but is normally baked in oval moulds and often has berries, coconut, chocolate and other ingredients added. You'll find them in Australia and New Zealand wherever a steaming soy latte is at large. French *friands*, puff pastry wrapped around a sausage, known as *'des cochons dans une couverture'* (pigs in a blanket) are thankfully no relation.

Back in Paris the best *financiers* for my money are to be found at Hugo & Victor in the 7th, Blé Sucré in the 12th, Gérad Mulot in the 6th, Des Gâteaux et du Pain in the 15th and at the boulangerie Moulin de la Vierge at various locations around the city.

FRIANDS FRAMBOISE D'AUSTRALIE

It takes a foolish man to stick his neck out and try to teach the French how to cook. I may be dragged kicking and screaming to the guillotine next time I dare show my face in Paris! However, I think that these financiers *or friands, as we call them down under, are a marked improvement on the sometimes bland, dry tea cakes you often find in Parisian pâtisseries. There is very little science to making a good friand, just quality ingredients and, of course, the real secret –* beurre noisette. *In Paris they bake them in dedicated gold bar-shaped* financier *tins and in Australia and New Zealand they make them in oval friand tins. If you don't have either of these, you can use small muffin tins instead.*

....

MAKES ABOUT 8

190 g (6¾oz) unsalted butter, ideally Charente, plus extra for greasing
150 g (5½ oz) fresh raspberries
200 g (7 oz) icing (confectioner's) sugar, plus extra for dusting
65 g (2 ⅓ oz) plain (all-purpose) flour
135 g (4¾ oz) ground almonds
6 egg whites
whipped cream or raspberry coulis, to serve

Preheat the oven to 180°C/350°F/gas mark 4 and generously butter 8 small loaf or oval *friand* tins. Lightly crush half the raspberries and set aside.

Make the *beurre noisette*. Heat the butter in a saucepan on a medium heat until it turns a golden brown and develops a nutty flavour – but be careful not to burn. Set aside to cool.

Sift the icing sugar, flour and almonds into a bowl and mix everything between your fingers.

Whisk the egg whites in another bowl until they form a light foam. Make a well in the centre of the dry ingredients and tip in the egg whites. Add the crushed raspberries then lightly stir in the melted golden butter to form a soft batter.

Divide evenly among the prepared tins. Scatter with the remaining raspberries and bake for 20 minutes. The *friands* are ready if they are just firm to the touch and golden brown and if a skewer inserted comes out clean. Stand for 5 minutes to cool in the tins before turning out on to a wire rack.

Dust with icing sugar and serve with thick whipped cream or raspberry coulis, if that's your thing.

2me. ARR^t.

RUE
DU CROISSANT

Tarte aux Pommes

~

Fruit tarts are what the French do best. They make them with precision and perfection using spirals of flawlessly cut fruit coated in a film of syrupy glaze, all arranged on a wafer-thin, slightly droopy pastry that is the envy of every domestic goddess. As you would expect, there is an abundance of mouth-watering fruit tarts on offer in Paris, often made to closely guarded recipes. But there is one tart that is nearly everyone's favourite – the Mother of all Tarts, the apple tart or *tarte aux pommes*. And it's probably the one your mother used to make. Deemed France's most popular dessert, its matriarchal mysteries have been passed down from generation to generation.

This timeless masterpiece has probably been around since pastry was invented. Combining tangy, juicy apples with crusty, sweet pastry seems the most logical marriage. It's sometimes known as *tarte normande* – a clue, perhaps, to a Normandy heritage? Smaller versions are known as *tartes fines* – as the name implies, they use a thinner pastry – and, of course, there is the terrific upside-down *Tarte Tatin* (see page 112). Even smaller, individual apple tarts are known by the diminutive *tartelletes aux pommes*.

The shortcrust pastry, or *pâte sucrée*, should be very French – sweet, crisp, thin and biscuity, not crumbly. And, naturally, it should be made with the best French butter and enriched with an egg yolk or two. In many cases a sweet, nutty frangipane layer is added as an extra filling, which really brings together the flavours. However, the more rustic versions do without this option and use extra layers of apples.

It goes without saying that the type of apples used dictates the type of tart you make, although the choice varies from recipe to recipe. Many pastry chefs prefer to stick with good old Granny Smiths for their balance of acidity and sweetness, and their ability to hold their shape when cooked, but really any firm-textured variety, cooker or eater, will do, such as Egremont Russets, Bramleys or Cox's Orange Pippin. Ultimately, what's needed is a variety that delivers meltingly succulent, brown-edged slices of apple that lightly caramelise in the cooking.

Tucking into a slice of *tarte aux pommes* straight from the ovens of a neighbourhood baker, or with a scoop of glace vanille in a sidewalk café, is to me one of the most redolent tastes of Paris. Having sampled a great many Parisian tarts over time, the rustic take on this time-honoured classic by the celebrated baker Poilâne, in the rue du Cherche-Midi, is my undisputed choice. Now managed by the youthful and spirited Apollonia Poilâne, their big chunks of browned, soft, sweet apple caramelised to perfection and encased in a randomly arranged but light, crunchy, slightly salty pastry is apple tart ecstasy.

Tarte aux
Abricots
Sur crème d'amandes

Prix : 22,30€

TRADITIONAL TARTE AUX POMMES

This is the evocative, good old-fashioned tarte aux pommes that French mothers and grandmothers used to bake for Sunday lunch — and hopefully still do. It is easy to make, but do take the time to arrange the apples on top so that they look the part. You can use any cooking or sweet apple but I prefer Granny Smiths.

. . . .

250 g (8¾ oz) ready-made shortcrust pastry (or see recipe on page 149 to make your own pâte sucrée)

FOR THE FRANGIPANE FILLING
100 g (3½ oz) unsalted butter, plus extra for greasing
50 g (1¾ oz) caster (superfine) sugar
100 g (3½ oz) ground almonds
2 large eggs

FOR THE APPLE FILLING
4 large Granny Smith apples, peeled, cored, halved and thinly sliced
50 g (1¾ oz) melted butter
½ egg, beaten

FOR THE GLAZE
4 tablespoons apricot jam
2 tablespoons water

Lightly grease a 23 cm (9 inch) fluted, removable-base tart tin. Remove the ready-made pastry from the fridge and stand at room temperature for 10 minutes. Roll out on a lightly floured surface to a 3 mm (¹/₁₀ inch) thickness and very carefully fit it to the tin, pressing down lightly. Make sure it takes the shape of the mould and covers the bottom of the tin entirely. When complete, prick the pastry base all over with a fork then put back in the fridge for at least 2 hours. This stops it from shrinking when baking.

Preheat the oven to 180°C/350°F/gas mark 4. Line the pastry base with parchment paper and fill with pie weights or uncooked beans or rice, and blind bake for 10 minutes. Remove the parchment and weights and continue cooking for another 10 minutes or until golden. Remove from the oven, leave to cool, then refrigerate.

For the frangipane filling, combine the butter and sugar until creamy, then fold in the ground almonds. Add the eggs and combine well. Spoon the frangipane filling into the tart case, being sure to smooth it evenly with a palette knife.

Starting from the outside, arrange the apple slices in a spiral pattern, overlapping one another until the entire surface is covered.

Bake for 25–30 minutes in a moderate oven, preheated to 160°C/325°F/gas mark 3. After 5 minutes, brush with the melted butter. Bake until the filling begins to brown, then 5 minutes before the end of the baking time, remove and brush the beaten egg over the top of the tart. Return to the oven for the remaining 5 minutes, until the apple edges start to caramelise slightly.

To make the glaze, heat the apricot jam with the water in a small pan, and sieve into a bowl. Remove the tart from the oven and, while still warm, use a pastry brush to generously cover the apples with the warm apricot glaze. Serve either hot or cold with crème fraîche or vanilla ice cream.

Chausson aux Pommes

~

After the *pain aux raisins* the *chausson aux pommes*, or apple turnover, is my next favourite. It's a semi-circular puff pastry *viennoiserie* virtuoso which, like many other similar *pâte feuilletée* pastries, probably originates in seventeenth-century France. Mention of a recipe for *chausson aux pommes* can be found in François Pierre de la Varenne's *'Le Cuisinier François'*, written in 1651, where it is described as a 'chubby-cheeked, neatly trimmed pastry stuffed with apple compote soaked in vanilla syrup'. Sounds spot on.

This folded apple pie has earned its place in French folklore. During the first weekend of September, the *pâtissiers*, bakers and confectioners in the city of St-Calais get together to celebrate the *Fête du Chausson* aux Pommes in commemoration of the chatelaine who, in 1630, saved the city from famine. In 1873 in Lemud, a commune in northeastern France, *chaussons aux pommes* were the size of a half pie – a pie crust folded in two and called *'conn-ché'*. It's believed these were the forerunner of today's *chausson aux pommes*, which is known as *gosette aux pommes* in Belgium.

Striking the right balance is the secret to a textbook *chausson aux pommes*. The play between the apple and *pâte feuilletée* is crucial. Perfection is a flaky, golden, multi-layered *pâte feuilletée* 'slipper' where the inner layers absorb the natural juicy acidity of the tart apple filling, which should be spicy, not too sweet, slightly crisp, chunky and oozing fruity deliciousness. Mushy, over-cooked apples are a crime, as are too much pastry crust or too much filling. And in no way should the sugar overpower. There should also be spicy hints of vanilla and cinnamon.

To distinguish between *chaussons aux pommes*, different primitive styles of decoration exist among its creators, from tree-like designs, herringbone patterns and simple slits to vent the steam from the apple compote. A glaze of brushed egg and sprinkled sugar is usually applied to give a final gloss.

As universal as the *chausson aux pommes* is in Paris, it is not always easy to discover excellence. Stohrer in the rue Montorgueil, the oldest pâtisserie in Paris, still bake theirs in the traditional method. If you are lucky enough to get one still warm from the oven then you are in for a treat. Blé Sucré will also knock your socks off. In the same league is the remarkable Christophe Vasseur at Du Pain et des Idées, who fills his *chaussons* with a whole, fresh apple so that the flavour burst is amazing. But again Des Gâteaux et du Pain does it for me with the best *chausson aux pommes* in Paris. Their *pâte feuilletée* is made with fresh butter, *Guérande* sea salt, and the filling combines a spicy mix of apple compote and roasted apples. Sublime.

CHAUSSON AUX POMMES

The secret to making this homey, comforting 'slipper' is getting the amount of apple filling just right for carefully folding into a simple pocket of puff pastry. Too little and it becomes a tasteless wedge of pastry, whereas too much and it will burst at the seams. The French often use Golden Delicious apples but this is not obligatory. For me, Granny Smiths always do the job better than most. Unless you have time on your hands, I recommend using a shop-bought puff pastry.

MAKES 4

4 Granny Smith apples
60 g (2¼ oz) caster
   (superfine) sugar, plus extra
   for sprinkling
pinch of salt
juice of ¼ lemon
15 g (½ oz) unsalted butter
½ teaspoon cinnamon
   powder
1 x 350 g (12 ⅓ oz) pack
   frozen puff pastry, thawed
   but cold
1 egg yolk, beaten, for egg
   wash

*FOR THE CINNAMON
CRÈME FRAÎCHE*
1 teaspoon cinnamon
   powder
3 tablespoons icing
   (confectioner's) sugar
250 ml (9 fl oz) crème fraîche

Preheat the oven to 200°C/400°F/gas mark 6. Peel and core the apples, and cut them into slices about 1.5 cm (½ inch) thick. Toss with the sugar and salt, then squeeze over the lemon juice. Mix together by hand.

Put the apples in a saucepan with the butter and cinnamon and simmer initially on a low heat until the apple releases its juices and the sugar dissolves. Then turn up to a medium-low heat until you start to reduce the liquid around the apples. Once they start to soften and are just about cooked, take off the heat and set aside to cool.

Roll out the puff pastry to 5 mm (⅕ inch) thick using a dusting of flour on the surface to prevent sticking and cut four circles the size of a saucer. Then roll out each circle to an oval shape about 3 mm (¹/₁₀ inch) thick.

Place a generous amount of the cooled cooked apple mixture on one half of each of the pastry ovals, being careful not to overstuff them. Use a pastry brush to paint the egg wash all along the rim of the pastry. Fold over into half moon shapes and press the edges together. It's best to crimp with a fork, or pastry crimper if you have one. Cut three small vents in the top of the pastry, brush the outside with the egg wash, and sprinkle with a little extra sugar.

Transfer the *chaussons* to a large baking sheet, and bake for 20 minutes until the pastry is golden, buttery and flaky, and the apples oozing and sweet.

Meanwhile, make the cinnamon *crème fraîche*: stir together the cinnamon powder, icing sugar and crème fraîche, and chill in the fridge.

Serve the *chaussons* warm with the chilled cinnamon *crème fraîche*.

5

Decadent Desserts

....

When it comes to sensational desserts Paris is the *nonpareil*. From succulent fruit tarts to indulgent, rich, sensual chocolate mousses, the French know how to seduce a weak-willed, sweet-toothed pudding fancier like me.

In the myriad restaurants, pâtisseries, tearooms and cafés of Paris, desserts take on many guises. It is sometimes hard to distinguish a dessert from a pastry – and, if the truth is known, there is probably no need to as they fulfil they same function, so to speak. These days desserts are no longer considered the crowning glory to the perfect meal – they are eaten by famished pleasure-seekers as self-indulgent snacks at any time of the day or night. As a result, the counters of Paris's pâtisseries, fine food stores and épiceries are festooned with every type of dessert you could dream of. Bought for lunch or dinner by hard-working Parisians too busy to spend time in the kitchen, they are also devoured by impulsive, hungry passers-by who can't suppress the desire for a taste of magic.

French desserts are such an extensive topic that, for the sake of brevity, I have limited this chapter to just a few Parisian classics, the ones I always lust after. So, without further ado, let's tuck into these popular Parisian puddings, legends in their own lunchtime.

~

Tarte Tatin and Mousse au Chocolat

⁓

Gorgeous, tarty, toffeed apple slices swimming in syrupy caramel under a divine duvet of layered puff pastry that absorbs the juices – does it get any better?

Supposedly, it all began back in the late nineteenth century at the family-run Hotel Tatin, just south of Paris. One story goes that Mme Stéphanie Tatin was making a conventional apple tart when she overcooked the apples. She attempted to rescue the dish by turning the tart upside down to stop the apples burning. Another account, possibly nearer the truth, is that she accidentally baked an apple tart the wrong way up, a mistake that resulted in the rich caramelised creation that has become the classic of today. Its popularity with the guests quickly made it the signature dish of the hotel – which still holds good to this day. However, its lasting legacy is probably due to Louis Vaudable, the Paris restaurateur, who made it a permanent fixture on the dessert menu at Maxim's de Paris.

Tarte Tatin is very rarely made well in restaurants – and unfortunately especially in Paris. They often they use the wrong apples, which results in a pulpy brown mess. Numerous pâtisseries make smaller, contemporary variants on the classic theme which can be delicious but don't really resemble the upside-down original. Des Gâteaux et du Pain do a particularly delicious one in a circular apple mould on a biscuity base that is topped with syrupy pecan nuts. Blé Sucré also turn out their visually stunning version comprising half a toffee apple on a flaky base, which is equally appetising. The *salon de thé* part of Berthillon on the Île Saint-Louis supposedly does a true *Tarte Tatin*, as does Lenôtre, but I confess I haven't tried either. To get the real thing you probably have to throw caution to the wind and head to Maxim's (or you could try the recipe overleaf).

Mousse au chocolat is another popular Parisian dessert with a devoted following, especially among children – of all ages. A sensuous symbiosis of whipped chocolate, eggs and butter, it's usually given a more contemporary treatment by Paris's creative pâtissiers, such that it rarely resembles the humble mousse of childhood memories. Gérard Mulot uses a combination of milk and dark chocolate mousse in his signature creation *'Coeur Frivole'* which is to die for, but not quite the genuine article. At Maison Caroline Savoy (daughter of celebrated chef Guy Savoy), you can buy a traditional, eggy *mousse au chocolat*-to-go in a resealable preserving jar. But purists will be hard pressed to find the time-honoured light and fluffy, yet at the same time thick and rich, über-choccy *mousse au chocolat* in Paris except at their favourite old-school bistro or café. If you have a bonne adresse, do let us in on it.

TRADITIONAL TARTE TATIN

This is the classic recipe with a few refinements. Contrary to what people say, you don't need a specialist Tarte Tatin tin to make it well, but it's all the better if you do. A heavy-bottomed, robust cast-iron or copper frying pan will do perfectly well, providing it can withstand cooking on the hob and in a very hot oven with molten caramelising sugar. Most recipes suggest a sweet eating apple, such as Cox's, but again I favour Granny Smiths as they are firm, have the right degree of acidity and hold together when cooked. Another good tip is to firmly press the pastry down on to the apples so they combine in the cooking.

. . . .

SERVES 6

350 g (12⅓ oz) ready-made puff pastry
5 medium Granny Smith apples
100 g (3½ oz) unsalted butter
160 g (5¾ oz) caster (superfine) sugar
½ teaspoon cinnamon powder

whipped cream, to serve

Preheat the oven to 200°C/400°F/gas mark 6. Select a suitable steel or copper frying pan ideally about 20 cm (8 inches) in diameter. Roll out the pastry until it is 3 mm (¹/₁₀ inch) thick and cut it into a round disc to fit as a lid a little bit wider than the pan. Cover the pastry with cling film so that it doesn't dry out and put in the fridge. Peel and core the apples and cut into halves lengthways.

Melt the butter and sugar together in the pan until they start to foam and begin to lightly caramelise.

Quickly place the apple halves cut side up in the caramel mixture, arranging them tightly together with a few small gaps, then sprinkle with cinnamon. Put a lid on the pan and cook over a low to medium heat for around 5–8 minutes, allowing the caramel to bubble up and over the apples until they are slightly soft, the caramel has started to turn a darker brown and you get a lovely toffee sauce.

Place the pastry circle on top of the apples, firmly tucking down the sides with a knife so that the edges reach the caramel in the pan.

Place on the top shelf of the oven and bake for 25–30 minutes until the pastry is golden-brown and well puffed up.

Remove from the oven and leave for an hour for the flavours to infuse. When ready to serve, put the pan back on the hob and gently reheat. Then put a serving dish over the pan and, holding it firmly in place, quickly flip upside down so that the pastry is underneath.

Serve with whipped cream.

RICH CHOCOLATE MOUSSE

Many traditional French chocolate mousse recipes are very heavy, using cream and butter, and are time-consuming to make. This is a straightforward version that calls for only three ingredients but results in a rich, intense chocolate flavour. It requires a bit of vigorous beating but it's well worth the effort. When making anything that uses uncooked eggs be sure to choose the freshest organic ones.

MAKES 4

120 g (4¼ oz) bittersweet
  dark chocolate
4 large eggs
25 g (1 oz) caster (superfine)
  sugar

Finely chop the chocolate with a sharp knife. Slowly melt it in a heatproof bowl set over a large pan of simmering water without allowing the bowl to touch the water. Stir gently until smooth and then remove from the heat.

Separate the egg yolks and whites into two clean bowls.

Whisk the egg whites with an electric beater, slowly folding in the sugar until the mixture forms soft peaks.

Add the egg yolks to the melted chocolate, beating vigorously with a wooden spoon until smooth. Be sure to allow the chocolate to cool just a few minutes before adding the yolks. If it's too hot the yolks will cook, and if it's too cold the mixture won't blend well.

Using a spatula, slowly fold one-quarter of the beaten egg whites into the chocolate mixture at a time, until completely incorporated – but don't overdo it or the mousse will lose volume.

Transfer the mousse to individual parfait glasses and refrigerate for at least 3 hours until set. Serve with a dollop of whipped cream.

Tarte au Chocolat

~

It doesn't get much more sublime than a French chocolate tart. A crusty, slightly sweet shortcrust shell filled to the brim with an intense, velvety-smooth glossy ganache. Rich, satisfying and sensual, it's just about everything you want from a dessert.

As an aside, the term 'ganache' is said to be the product of a happy accident, when some time in the mid-nineteenth century a chocolatier's apprentice inadvertently poured boiling cream into some molten chocolate. The fuming *maître chocolatier* cursed his apprentice, calling him '*ganache*', a term that at the time meant something like stupid or horse's arse in French. As it turned out, the silky, chocolatey creamy end result was divine, but the unfortunate apprentice's nickname stuck, and luckily so did his invention which today is at the core of fine chocolate-making the world over. It's an amusing anecdote but probably one that, like chocolate itself, has been richly embellished over time.

Frequently when '*flâneuring*' about the lesser-known *quartiers* of Paris, I have sought stimulation from those seemingly uncomplicated, individual *tartes au chocolat* found in nearly every reputable pâtisserie that titillates the streets. They pack such a passionate flavour burst of chocolatey deliciousness that they immediately put a spring in your step and a Charles Aznavour song in your heart.

La Maison du Chocolat is famed for their petite yet condensed chocolate tarts in a perfect *pâte sucrée* shell, which can be purchased at their numerous stores around Paris. You can also bank on Gérard Mulot on the Left Bank to be on the money. His divine chocolate tart is worth every cent and is decorated with a bling of gold leaf to give that added *je ne sais quoi*. That grand master of all things cacao, Jean-Paul Hévin, does a stylish multi-layered *tartelette au chocolat* that has three types of ganache filling and is crowned with a crisp, sugar-coated *croustillant*. Thank Hévin for little chocolate tarts…

BITTERSWEET TARTE AU CHOCOLAT

I frequently make this sumptuous chocolate tart as my 'wow' factor dinner-party dessert. It's relatively easy and nearly always elicits the desired amount of 'ooohs' and 'aaahs' from my guests.

. . . .

SERVES 6

250 g (9 oz) ready-made shortcrust pastry (or see recipe on page 149 to make your own pâte sucrée)

FOR THE CHOCOLATE GANACHE
200 g (7 oz) bittersweet chocolate
250 ml (9 fl oz) double (heavy) cream
1 vanilla pod
100 g (3½ oz) caster (superfine) sugar
25 g (1 oz) unsalted butter, diced, plus extra for greasing

Lightly grease a 23 cm (9 inch) fluted, removable-base tart tin. Remove the ready-made pastry from the fridge and stand at room temperature for 10 minutes. Roll out on a lightly floured surface to a 3 mm ($1/10$ inch) thickness and very carefully fit it to the tin, pressing down lightly. Make sure it takes the shape of the mould and covers the bottom of the tin entirely. When complete, prick the pastry base all over with a fork then put back in the fridge for at least 2 hours. This stops it from shrinking when baking.

Preheat the oven to 180°C/350°F/gas mark 4. Line the pastry base with parchment paper and fill with pie weights or uncooked beans or rice, and blind bake for 10 minutes. Remove the parchment and weights and continue cooking for another 10 minutes or until golden. Remove from the oven, leave to cool, then refrigerate.

To make the chocolate ganache: finely chop the chocolate, transfer to a heatproof bowl and set aside. Pour the cream into a saucepan, then split the vanilla pod and scrape out the seeds and along with the pod add to the cream. Add the sugar and bring to the boil for about 30 seconds, stirring gently to dissolve the sugar, then fish out the vanilla pod. Slowly pour into the chocolate and let it melt for about 1 minute. Then start to gently whisk in a circular motion, starting from the middle and working outwards, to achieve a smooth texture. Gradually add the butter, whisking continuously until the ganache is silky smooth and shiny.

When the chocolate is completely dissolved with the cream and butter and still warm but not hot, remove the tin with the pastry from the fridge and pour in the ganache. Leave to cool, then chill for 2 hours. Remove the tart from the tin when solid, and serve with whipped cream or vanilla ice cream.

CLASSIC PARISIAN BISTRO CRÈME BRÛLÉE

Back in the seventeenth century François Massialot, chef de cuisine to various illustrious personages, was credited with inventing the crème brûlée, *in which the 'burnt' sugar topping was melted with a red-hot fire shovel. This classic creamy, Parisian bistro dessert is another firm favourite, providing it's not adulterated with things like fruit or chocolate. To me, it's all about thick, vanilla-infused custard and glossy shards of crunchy sugar. The easiest way to caramelise the sugar topping is with a chef's blowtorch but, if you don't have one, the alternative is to place the ramekins as near to the heat as possible under a very hot grill — but keep your eye on them. And do remember to leave them to sit for a while in order to let the top harden and the ramekins cool down.*

....

SERVES 6

600 ml (20 fl oz) double (heavy) cream
2 fat vanilla pods
8 egg yolks
30 g (1 oz) caster (superfine) sugar
6 tablespoons soft brown sugar

Preheat the oven to 160°C/325°F/gas mark 3. Pour the cream into a saucepan with a lid. Split the vanilla pods lengthways and scrape the seeds into the cream and then add the pods. Bring just to the boil and simmer for a few minutes, then turn off the heat and pop on the lid. Leave to infuse for 15 minutes.

Beat the egg yolks with the sugar in a large heatproof bowl until pale and creamy. Bring the cream back to boiling point, fish out the vanilla pods, then add the egg mixture. Turn down the heat and constantly whisk until the mixture starts to thicken and you have a smooth, custard-like consistency. It mustn't boil otherwise the eggs will curdle.

Pour into six 150 ml (5 fl oz) ovenproof ramekins until two-thirds full.

Sit the ramekins in a bain-marie - a large roasting tray at least 8 cm (3 inches) deep – and pour in enough hot water to come three-quarters of the way up the sides of the ramekins. Place on the middle shelf of the oven and cook for 35–40 minutes until the *crèmes brûlées* are set but a bit wobbly in the middle. Remove from the water and allow to cool before placing them in the fridge.

An hour before you're ready to serve, sprinkle one level tablespoon of brown sugar over the surface of each one, then caramelise either with a blowtorch or under a very fierce preheated grill until golden and bubbling. Leave to cool for a few minutes, and then pop back in the fridge until dessert time.

6

Ice Cream, Gelato and Sorbet

....

Rome is allegedly the ice-cream capital of the world, but in my humble opinion Paris can justifiably claim to be a close second. If the Italians didn't actually invent ice cream then there is no question that they perfected it. However, and without wanting to offend my Italian friends, I would say that I have often had better ice cream in Paris than I have in Italy — and that's coming from an addict who simply adores the stuff. I join with other ice-cream *aficionados* who think that Berthillon has some of the best *glace* on this globe but equally you can now find some of the best Italian *gelato* in the City of Light.

These days, like many Parisians, my loyalties are divided between the long-established classical French *glace* and the recent vogue for Italian *gelato*. Old-style artisanal French *glaciers* make an intense, rich *glace* using cream and eggs which freezes into a harder, more concentrated consistency. For my part, I love the dense, smooth texture and the more conventional Paris *parfums* — think *marron glacé* or *caramel beurre salé* made by *glaciers* such as Raimo, who have a long tradition of making ice cream in the conventional French style.

In recent years Italian *gelaterias* have been popping up all over the city, as Parisians and visitors alike display a preference for the lighter, more delicate *gelato* textures. *Glace* purists, however, consider these little more than inferior Italian frozen custard; whereas real *gelato aficionados* prefer their ices made with whole milk and believe they shouldn't contain cream or eggs, even though many modern producers are now using these ingredients in an attempt to make their *gelato* more creamy and intense. This narrowing of the differences sometimes makes it hard to distinguish between a *glace* and a *gelato* — they are both delicious in their own right. But still the battle for the hearts and palates of Parisian ice-cream connoisseurs rages on.

As you would expect, Parisian sorbets are equally sensuous, with a mind-boggling assortment of fresh fruit tastes that leave little to the imagination. Concentrated, full-on flavours that don't resort to anything artificial are an art form which has become refined in this town among the sorbet-making elite. A little goes a long way. What could be more sublime than a recent experience I had in Paris? Enjoying an intense fresh strawberry sorbet, I stood on a bridge over the river Seine on a warm summer's night listening to the sounds of someone playing a saxophone down on the quay. Pure magic!

～

Glace or Gelato?

Legend has it that the teenage Florentine noblewoman Catherine de Medici, who became Queen Consort of France when she married Henry II in 1533, introduced ice cream to Paris from Italy. The first French recipe for 'flavoured ices' appeared in a book written by pharmacist Nicholas Lémery around 1674. More recipes featured in a 1692 cookbook by chef François Massialot: his concoctions reputedly resulted in a coarse, gravel-like texture, a far cry from the creamy *glaces* of today.

Much has been written or blogged about the historic emporium, Maison Berthillon. Opened in 1954 and situated on the Île Saint-Louis, you couldn't find a more charismatic location to enjoy ice cream. At last count this glorious *glacier* had around 36 *parfums* of their delectable homemade ice cream plus 30-odd sensational sorbet flavours. They use only natural ingredients, and a favourite among Parisians is the *fraises des bois*, but if it's available do try the exceptional *'Glace Tatin'* – sumptuous vanilla and caramel ice cream infused with caramelised apples. The owners, descendants of the eponymous Monsieur Berthillon, are so confident of their loyal following that they close up for a number of weeks in the summer – the peak ice-cream season – and join the rest of France on holiday. But, fear not, a number of their ice creams are available in other cafés, tearooms and restaurants displaying the Berthillon logo.

Just up the street in the rue Saint-Louis-en-l'Île is the entrepreneurial Italian *gelato* chain Amorino, also found at other locations in Paris. Their colourful, floral-styled cones, which are spatula created not scooped, offer a cacophony of exotic flavours such as *frutto della passione* or, my favourite, *cioccolato al latte di soia bio*. From here, cross the Pont Marie to the rue de Roi de Sicile in the Marais and you will find an equally good, if not better, genuine Italian *gelato* at Pozzetto. Their emerald-green pistachio uses Sicilian nuts and they do a really wonderful *zabaione*, made from egg yolks, sugar and Marsala wine.

The much-fêted Raimo out in the 12th is well worth the trip to the east side of Paris just to sit outside and experience their flowery tributes, including *lavande*, rose and *violette*. Another *gelato* favourite of mine is authentic *gelataria* Deliziefollie in the rue Montorgueil who also have to be in the first division of Italian ice-cream parlours. The all-natural *glace* at Le Bac à Glaces in the rue du Bac results in some attention-grabbing flavours – try their avocado ice cream. And Martine Lambert in rue Cler in the 7th is also one of the better traditional ice-cream parlours in Paris. Finally, it's worth flagging that many pâtisseries, chocolatiers and *confiseurs* make their own delicious ice creams. La Maison du Chocolat, Pierre Hermé, Blé Sucré, Kayser and À la Mère de Famille are just a few.

FRENCH-STYLE RICH DARK CHOCOLATE ICE CREAM

Here's an easy recipe for a really rich, sensationally creamy French-style glace, which, like chez Berthillon, will get people queuing for more. It's a lot easier if you have an ice-cream maker but, if you don't, be prepared to do a bit of stirring.

. . . .

SERVES 4

125 g (4½ oz) bittersweet dark chocolate
1 vanilla pod or 2 teaspoons vanilla extract
225 ml (7½ fl oz) whole milk
5 egg yolks
75 g (2¾ oz) caster (superfine) sugar
1 tablespoon cocoa powder
200 ml (7 fl oz) double (heavy) cream

Using a sharp knife, carefully chop the chocolate into small pieces about 5 mm (⅕ inch) in size and put to one side.

Next make the custard base: cut open and scrape the seeds from the vanilla pod, then add them along with the pod to the milk in a saucepan. Bring slowly to the boil, then leave aside for a few minutes to cool and for the vanilla to infuse.

In a mixing bowl, beat together the egg yolks and sugar until thick and pale in colour. Fish out the vanilla pod then slowly pour the hot but not boiling milk into the mixture, stirring until it is well mixed.

Pour the mixture back into the saucepan, add the cocoa powder and heat very gently while continuing to stir with a wooden spoon until the custard thickens – but be careful not to bring to the boil. When the custard coats the back of the wooden spoon, remove the saucepan from the heat. Stir in the chopped chocolate pieces. Keep stirring until all the chocolate has melted. Leave to cool. When it's completely cool, lightly whip the cream and fold into the chocolate mixture.

Churn in an ice-cream maker if you have one. If not, freeze in a metal bowl or suitable container, and stir every 15 minutes while freezing to stop ice crystals forming. Finally, if you used an ice-cream maker, spoon into a container and freeze until firm.

HOMEMADE BLACKCURRANT SORBET WITH CASSIS

This time-honoured French sorbet is simple to make and creates a great after-dinner interlude before the cheese and a serious pudding. The cassis gives it some real oomph and somehow makes it taste more French. It is best made with fresh blackcurrants when they are in season — but you will find frozen ones have lots of flavour too. If available serve with fresh blackcurrants on top. Be sure to take the sorbet out of the freezer twenty minutes before serving.

. . . .

SERVES 6

450 g (1 lb) fresh or frozen
*   blackcurrants*
150 ml (5 fl oz) water
30 g (1 oz) caster (superfine)
*   sugar*
1 egg white (optional)
5 tablespoons cassis

Wash and de-stalk the blackcurrants. Put them with the water and sugar in a saucepan and simmer gently for 4–5 minutes until just soft. It is crucial that you don't 'cook' the blackcurrants, so take them off the heat the moment they start to burst.

Blend together using a wooden spoon and push through a sieve.

Pour the purée into an ice-cream machine and churn until frozen, or freeze in a suitable container in the freezer, whisking the sorbet with a fork every 15 minutes to break up the crystals until it has a creamy consistency.

If you're not using an ice-cream maker, you can make the sorbet lighter by adding an egg white before the mixture freezes completely. Using an electric beater, whisk the egg white until stiff and fold into the semi-frozen blackcurrant purée to make a fluffy mixture. Pour back into the container and freeze again until solid.

7

Confiserie – Favourite Parisian Confectionery

···

Confectionery is a loose term applying to nearly everything made with sugar but here I'm referring to what the British call sweets, the Americans candy, the Australians lollies and the French *confiseries*. Confusingly, they also call them *bonbons*. Since the introduction of sugar in French cuisine, the country's cooks have been conjuring up all manner of *confiserie*, and there is no doubt that other cultures have influenced them to a great extent. The *petit four* appears a very French invention but its origins are oriental. *Calissons*, which are a traditional candy from Aix-en-Provence, came originally from Italy, *nougat* from Persia and *dragées*, sugared almonds, probably from Greece.

Although most *confiseries* in Paris come from different regions of France they have all gravitated to the capital, home to some of the most sublime sweets on the planet, from old-fashioned, hard-boiled jaw-breakers, succulent, soft fruit jellies (*pâtes de fruits*), sugary candied fruits, and lip-smacking liquorice to marshmallows, fudges, toffees and the ever-popular caramels.

Paris offers connoisseurs of confectionery a select number of very special places to visit and first on your list should be the historic *confiserie*, À la Mère de Famille, on the rue de Faubourg Montmartre in the colourful 9th. Established in 1761, it is one of the most enchanting shops in Paris, with its mosaic tiled floor, mahogany *vitrines*, vintage cashier's kiosk, beautiful chandeliers and age-old exterior adorned with antique signage. It is named after Marie Adelaïde Bridault, mother of four, who in 1807 took over the business when her husband died and developed it into a household name. Probably the oldest sweet shop in Europe, it has an irresistible choice of classic *confiserie* and specialities, such as their candied fruits, *marrons glacés*, *calissons*, caramels and *guimauve*. They are equally known for their enticing selection of chocolates and *nouveautés*, as well as their memorable ice cream – try the mint chocolate.

Then there is the unforgettable *confiserie*-cum-*chocolatier*, L'Étoile d'Or, in Montmartre, owned by the wonderfully passionate and eccentric Denise Acabo – an experience not to be missed. And for a tour of France by its regional *confiserie*, visit the delightfully charismatic Georges at Le Bonbon au Palais in the 5th. His pralines from Mazet are the best in France.

Faced with such bounty, I am going to be completely single-minded and focus on three of my favourites: *marrons glacés*, *pâte de fruits* and *caramel au beurre salé*.

∼

Marrons Glacés and Pâte de Fruits

~

Who can resist these glazed crystallised chestnut confectioneries candied in sugar syrup when cavorting in the French capital? They're the height of indulgence: subtly sweet, rich, nutty, gooey morsels of vanillary delectation that come wrapped in that gorgeous gold paper you can't help licking to savour every drop of sticky deliciousness. Be warned, though: due to their seasonality and painstaking preparation (each *marron glacé* takes about four days to make), they cost the earth but for my money they're worth every cent.

The idea to crystallise chestnuts probably came from Piedmont in Italy in the sixteenth century, but, like so many delicacies, they were ultimately refined in France. Close to the best chestnut-producing areas, Lyon has been the centre of the *marron glacé* trade for the last 300 years. Clément Faugier, an engineer better known for designing bridges, is credited with modernising the making of *marrons glacés* in the nineteenth century. He established a flourishing industry in the Rhône-Alpes centre of gastronomy which has survived until today

Finding good *marrons glacés* in Paris is not difficult but only in the right season – October through March. They are traditionally eaten at Christmas and New Year and so sell out fast. Pierre Hermé, along with La Maison du Chocolat, do some of the best in Paris, as do Fauchon. And a visit to Hédiard in La Madeleine is a must even if you're not in the market for a *marron*. But if you do want to shell out for these golden goodies (not that old chestnut), go to À la Mère de Famille and enjoy the experience of shopping at this vintage sweet shop.

Pâte de fruits, meaning fruit paste or fruit jellies, are a French *spécialité* that probably dates back to the Dark Ages. They're full-on, fruit-flavoured, funky-coloured, sweet 'n' sour chewy confections that stick to the teeth and deliver a sensorial sugar rush. Their multi-coloured, jewel-like presentation in the counters of the capital's high-end *confiseurs*, chocolatiers and gourmet stores is a joy to behold. Made from concentrated, or more accurately reduced, puréed fresh fruit combined with gelatine and heaps of cane sugar and then sprinkled with a speciality 'sanding' sugar, the flavours of these pectin-packed little nuggets trespass into the exotic. Apart from the common-or-garden fruits, it's difficult to choose between mango, mirabelle, morello cherry, passion fruit, pineapple, quince, lychee, clementine, coconut, blackcurrant or fig, to name but a few.

Where can you pick up the best *pâte de fruits* in Paris? Jacques Genin, in his pristine place in the Marais, sells his jellied gems in a handsome, monogrammed aluminium tin. Patrick Roger makes an equally delicious cube of candy, but for the fruitiest, purest flavours in town head for Fauchon or Hédiard in place de la Madeleine.

CHOCOLATE-DIPPED DRIED FRUIT

This is an easy recipe for beautiful after-dinner petits fours that look exquisite and taste divine. You can use any dried fruit that's available locally: prunes, apricots, figs, kiwi fruit, dates, pineapple — whatever takes your fancy. The secret is in tempering the chocolate. I know this strikes terror into the hearts of many, but don't be put off: if you're going to be making chocolates regularly, invest in a chocolate thermometer. They're not expensive and make it so much easier to accurately temper chocolate. It's all about keeping your cool...

MAKES ABOUT 20

20 or so mixed dried fruit
100 g (3½ oz) bittersweet dark chocolate
100 g (3½ oz) milk chocolate

Cut up both lots of chocolate into even chunks.

Place about two-thirds of the chocolate in a heatproof bowl on top of a saucepan filled with about 5 cm (2 inches) water, making sure that the bottom of the bowl is not touching the water. Allow the chocolate to melt slowly.

As soon as it has melted, turn off the heat, remove the bowl from the pan and wrap a clean tea towel around the base to keep it warm. Add the remaining chocolate, stick in the thermometer and, keeping it in, stir until the mixture cools down to 31–32°C (88–90°F). Once it reaches this temperature, it's ready to use.

Line a large baking tray with aluminium foil. When the chocolate reaches the right temperature, dip the dried fruit into the mixture using small tongs or chopsticks, taking care not to immerse fully so that you still recognise part of the fruit.

Place the dipped fruit on the prepared tray and leave to cool at room temperature. Ideally, the chocolate coating should have a glossy sheen.

Caramels

The craze for this guilty pleasure continues in Paris with a fervent passion: so much so that I was tempted to include caramels in the chapter on fashions and fads. However, I doubt that the French love of this classic *confiserie* has ever gone away. French children of all ages have been chewing these toffee sweets since they were invented in the Middle Ages. Brittany, famous for its butter, cream and *fleur de sel* (sea salt), seems to be the agreed birthplace of this popular treat, especially in its most recent incarnation — *le caramel au beurre salé*, salted butter caramel, that is currently all the rage. Classic salted caramels have been on sale in France since the nineteenth century, famously from the Île de Ré, in their established blue and gold tins.

Despite the fact that the decadent mix of sugar, cream and butter has for centuries been in the repertoire of chefs from all over the continent, the addition of *fleur de sel* seems to diminish the level of guilt associated with eating something so wickedly sweet. And *le caramel au beurre salé* is very sweet. But that little bit of defiant salt is the salvation that makes indulging in this idiosyncratic Breton *bonbon* acceptable for those guilt-ridden Parisians. Because of this redeeming quality, *le caramel au beurre salé* is now used as an ingredient in virtually anything sweet in Paris: ice creams, *macarons* (check out Pierre Hermé's creation), desserts, pastries and cocktails — it has even impregnated scented candles. Where will it all end?

Getting your fix of *caramel au beurre salé* in Paris is not too challenging. Every quality *confiseur*, chocolatier and purveyor of all things sweet has jumped on the bandwagon. The best bet for the softer, more buttery type is Jacques Genin in the Haut Marais, with flavours such as passion fruit-mango, cinnamon, pistachio, liquorice and plenty others. And for the more traditional Breton caramel, go up to Montmartre to L'Étoile d'Or, the unforgettable *confiserie*-cum-chocolatier where the delightful Denise Acabo sells the celebrated *caramel au beurre salé* from the most respected *confiseur* in the country, Henri Le Roux. As she will inform you when she fervently grips your arm in that exuberant Gallic gesture used to emphasise a point, *'Ils sont orgasmiques'*. You can also find the very same at Georges Le Bonbon au Palais. Meert is another traditional *confiseur* with an intriguing heritage that sells a range of different caramels at their charming 'new' shop on the corner of rue Elzévir and rue du Parc Royal in the Marais.

CLASSIC CARAMEL AU BEURRE SALÉ

This recipe makes genuine French caramels almost identical to those found in the famous Paris confiseurs. It pays to be attentive and stir well during cooking, as it can create certain 'hot spots' in the pan and cook very quickly. You can use salted or unsalted butter, but if you only have unsalted just add an extra pinch of salt. Be aware, though — a sugar thermometer is essential.

. . . .

MAKES ABOUT 24

200 ml (7 fl oz) double (heavy) cream
80 g (2¾ oz) salted butter, diced, at room temperature, plus extra for greasing
1 teaspoon vanilla extract
1 level teaspoon sea salt, preferably French fleur de sel
160 g (5⅔ oz) golden syrup
200 g (7 oz) caster (superfine) sugar

Line a 23 cm (9 inch) loaf tin with baking paper and lightly grease with butter. In a small saucepan heat the cream with half of the butter. Add the vanilla extract and sea salt and bring to the boil. Remove from the heat, cover with a lid and keep warm.

In another medium-size, heavy-duty saucepan, heat the golden syrup with the sugar, stirring gently until smooth.

Continue to heat the syrup until it reaches 155°C (310°F), using a sugar thermometer to check. To get an accurate reading, tilt the saucepan to make sure the bulb of the thermometer is fully submerged in the syrup.

Leave in the thermometer and turn the heat right down before slowly stirring in the warm cream until the mixture is smooth.

Turn up the heat again until the mixture reaches 127°C (260°F), again using the thermometer to check.

Take out the thermometer, remove the saucepan from the heat and thoroughly stir in the remaining butter until it's all melted and the mixture is smooth. Pour into the prepared loaf tin and place on a rack until completely cool, then lift out the caramel, peel back the baking paper and, taking great care, slice the bar into cubes with a sharp knife.

Wrap the caramels in waxed paper. They'll keep for almost a month in an airtight container.

1

2

3

4

5

6

7

HOW TO MAKE PERFECT
PASTRY THE FRENCH WAY

I know making pastry isn't everyone's idea of fun, so this is for all those dedicated bakers who enjoy a challenge. But there's no shame in cheating by using a ready-made shortcrust or puff pastry. French pâtissiers tend to use four different types of pastry: pâte feuilletée (puff pastry), mainly for viennoiseries; pâte brisée (literally broken dough), mainly for savoury recipes; pâte sucrée (sweet dough), made with icing sugar and suitable for fruit tarts and pies; and, finally, pâte sablée (sandy dough), for flans and tarts — made in a slightly different way to pâte sucrée, it is the richest of all pastries, sometimes has ground almonds and is flavoured with vanilla. Faced with this baffling choice, you will find that this rich, sweet shortcrust pastry recipe (a version of pâte sucrée) is a good base for the apple, strawberry and chocolate tart recipes in this book, as well as many others.

MAKES A BLIND-BAKED TART CASE APPROXIMATELY 24 CM (9½ INCHES) IN DIAMETER AND 2–3 CM (1 INCH) DEEP, PLUS SOME EXTRA

200 g (7 oz) plain (all-purpose) flour, plus extra for dusting
pinch of sea salt
75 g (2¾ oz) caster (superfine) sugar
90 g (3 oz) unsalted butter, diced and chilled
2 egg yolks, at room temperature

1 Sift the flour, sea salt into a large mixing bowl. Add the sugar.

2 Work the flour and sugar into the butter by rubbing them together with your fingers until completely combined. Make sure you incorporate lots of air by continually lifting up the mixture and letting it fall back, until it resembles fine breadcrumbs.

3 Using a round-bladed knife, thoroughly mix the egg yolks into the mixture.

4 Next, with a flat-bladed knife or your hands, work the mix to form a soft dough.

5 On a lightly floured work surface, briefly knead the dough with your hands until smooth. Wrap the pastry in cling film and chill for 30 minutes. (Alternatively, it can be frozen for use at a later date.)

6 Preheat the oven to 180°C/350°F/gas mark 4. Lightly sprinkle a rolling pin and work surface with flour and evenly roll out the chilled pastry until it is large enough to fit your tart tin and is about 3–4 mm (⅙ inch) thick.

7 Wrap the pastry around the rolling pin and then unfold it over a lightly greased tart tin, making sure it is centred. Gently push the pastry to snugly fit the shape of the tin. Trim away any excess with a knife and prick the bottom with a fork. Place in the fridge for at least 2 hours to stop shrinkage when baking.

8 Remove from the fridge, line the pastry base with parchment paper and fill with pie weights or uncooked beans or rice, and blind bake for 10 minutes. Remove the parchment and weights and continue cooking for another 10 minutes or until golden. Remove from the oven, cool on a rack, then refrigerate until you need it.

Bonnes Adresses à Paris

These are some of my favourite addresses in Paris that I want to share with you. They are some of the best chocolatiers, patisseries, confiseries and salons de thé in town. It is not a definitive list but rather those places where I love to shop or visit. For opening hours, check the websites or call ahead.

MY TOP 10 PARIS GREATS

Pierre Hermé

72 rue Bonaparte, 75006 Paris
+33 (0)1 43 54 47 77
Métro: Saint-Sulpice
www.pierreherme.com
Famous for his delectable macarons he is also a master chocolatier, *confiseur* and the best *patissier* in Paris, as well as creating his own contemporary desserts all renowned for their extraordinary flavour marriages that have become exclusively his signature. He has various boutiques in Paris.

Patrick Roger

108 blvd. Saint-Germain, 75006 Paris
+33 (0)1 43 29 38 42
Métro: Odéon
www.patrickroger.com
The 'wild child' of chocolate M Roger is my favourite *maitre chocolatier* in France with the some of the most sublime taste sensations I have ever experienced. With five boutiques in Paris it is not hard to indulge in his delights.

Gérard Mulot

76 rue de Seine, 75006 Paris
+33 (0)1 43 26 85 77
Métro: Odéon
www.gerard-mulot.com
Principally a Parisian *patissier* whose busy boutique also displays a wonderful selection of chocolates and *confiserrie*, as well as other goodies with some very special seasonal offerings, especially at Easter. M Mulot is a must if you are on the left bank.

Blé Sucré

7 rue Antoine Vollon, 75012 Paris
+33 (0)1 43 40 77 73
Métro: Ledru-Rollin
The charming Fabrice Le Bourdat and his wife run one of the best small neighbourhood unpretentious patisseries in Paris not far from Bastille. His madeleines have a cult following and his croissants are equally good, but everything is outstanding. Blé Sucré must be on your list!

Des Gâteaux et du Pain

63 boulevard Pasteur, 75015 Paris
+33 (0)1 45 38 94 16
Métro: Pasteur
www.desgateauxetdu pain.com
Mme Claire Damon is a genius having worked with Pierre Hermé and other greats. Her patisserie creations demonstrate her unique skills capturing the spirit of the classics which she gives a contemporary spin. Check the *viennoiserie* too - some of the best in Paris. Well worth a trip to the 15th.

Du Pain et des Idées

34 rue Yves Toudic, 75010 Paris
+33 (0)1 42 40 44 52
Métro:République or Jacques Bonsergent
www. dupainetdesidees. com
Run by the talented Christophe Vasseur, an award-winning French baker who was named the Baker of the Year by Gault-Millau, this beautiful old neighbourhood boulangerie near the canal St Martin with its cheerful staff is indeed filled with 'bread and ideas'. Try the heavenly *chausson aux pomme*, banana *pain au chocolat* or their many variations on the *pain aux raisin…* but get there early.

Pain de Sucre

14 rue Rambuteau, 75003 Paris
+33 (0)1 45 74 68 92
Métro: Rambuteau
www. patisseriepaindesucre. com
An adventurous patisserie in the Marais quarter with a cult following specialising in melt-in-the-mouth marshmallows or *guimauve*. Sample the *fleur d'orange*. It also pushes out the envelopes on more classical pastries with exotic flavours and imaginative use of fruit. A must is the wacky *baba au rhum* and the *pain d'epice*.

Bonnes Adresses à Paris

Poilâne
8 rue du Cherche-Midi, 75006 Paris
+33 (0)1 45 48 42 59
Métro: Sèvres Babylone
www.poilane.fr
This world-renowned bakery not only has some of the best bread in Paris but also a fabulous selection of irresistible *viennoiserie* including a rustic, cinnamon apple tart to die for and their famous sable '*punitions*' (punishments). Visit the flagship Saint-Germain-des-Prés bakery or other shops around Paris.

À La Mère de Famille
34–35 rue de Faubourg Montmartre, 75009 Paris
+33 (0)1 47 70 83 69
Metro: Cadet, Le Peletier or Grands-Boulevards
www.lameredefamille. com
A visit to Paris's oldest and most beautiful *confiserie* and chocolatier, founded in 1761 and still operating in its original location, is a journey into the past. They also do an amazing chocolate ice cream.

Carette
4 place du Trocadero, 75016 Paris
+33 (0)1 47 27 98 85
25 Place des Vosges, 75003 Paris
+33 (0)1 48 87 94 07
www.carette-paris.com
This patisserie and *salon de thé* is a Paris institution patronised by the *haut monde*. I prefer their Place des Vosges tea salon as it is such a great setting and not so crowded. Try their award-winning éclairs. Breakfast at the Trocadero location is a must, however, with a stunning view of the Eiffel Tower.

MY OTHER FAVOURITE CHOCOLATIERS

Debauve et Gallais
30 rue des Saints Pères, 75007 Paris
+33 (0)1 45 48 54 67
Métro: St-Germain-des-Prés
www.debauveandgallais. com
Probably the oldest chocolate shop in Paris appointed by the King of France even though France has been a republic since 1792. Balzac, Proust and Brillat-Savarin bought their bonbons here!

Jacques Genin
133, rue de Turenne, 75003 Paris
+33 (0)1 45 77 29 01
Métro: République or Filles du Calvaire
M Genin chocolatier and patissier extraordinaire should really be in my top 10. His modern salon in the haut Marais showcasing his outstanding creations is worth a visit just for his caramel *millefeuille*.

Jean-Charles Rochoux
16 rue d'Assas, 75006 Paris
+33 (0)1 42 84 29 45
Métro: Rennes
www.jcrochoux.fr
Another classic Parisian artisan chocolatier creating superb bonbons and chocolate bars with beautiful packaging. Try his bar filled with whole hazelnuts encased in crunchy caramel.

Jean-Paul Hévin
231 rue Saint-Honoré, 75001 Paris
+33 (0)1 55 35 35 96
Métro: Concorde, Tuileries
www.jphevin.com
A number of boutiques about Paris where you find quality ingredients and superb creativity when it comes to shapes and flavours. Great hot chocolate too in his upstairs 'chocolate bar' in the rue Saint-Honoré.

La Maison du Chocolat
52 rue François 1er, 75008 Paris
+33 (0)1 47 23 38 25
Métro: George V
www. lamaisonduchocolat.com
The world-famous chocolate-maker, with many locations around Paris. Full-on hot chocolate – but not for the faint-hearted.

Michel Cluizel
201 rue Saint-Honoré, 75001 Paris
+33 (0)1 42 44 11 66
Métro: Tuileries
www.cluizel.com
Now run by his daughter Catherine, this classic Paris chocolate landmark has a wonderful selection of diverse bars and bonbons.

Pierre Marcolini
89 rue de Seine, 75006 Paris
+33 (0)1 44 07 39 07
Métro: Mabillon
www.marcolini.com
A famous Belgian chocolatier with

that special French refinement. Great ganaches such as Earl Grey Tea.

Pralus

35 rue Rambuteau, 75004 Paris
+33 (0)1 48 04 05 05
Métro: Rambuteau
www.chocolats-pralus.com
François Pralus, is a chocolate adventurer offering exotic bars and bonbons with chocolate from around the world. Try his 'Praluline', a delectable praline-filled brioche, or the chocolate Tropical Pyramids.

MY OTHER FAVOURITE PATISSERIES

Sadaharu Aoki

35 rue de Vaugirard, 75006 Paris
+33 (0)1 45 44 48 90
Métro: Rennes
www.sadaharuaoki.com
An incredibly talented patissier who puts a Japanese spin on his delectable creations. Try his sesame éclair or *Opéra au thé vert*. Three boutiques in Paris.

Dalloyau

101, rue du Faubourg Saint-Honoré, 75008 Paris
+33 (0)1 42 99 90 00
Métro:Saint-Philippe du Roule, Franklin Roosevelt
www.dalloyau.fr
An institution with boutiques all over Paris. Home of the *L'Opera* gateaux and other delicacies.

Hugo & Victor

40 boulevard Raspail, 75007 Paris
+33 (0)1 44 39 97 73
Métro: Sèvres Babylone
www.hugovictor.com
A fairly recent addition to the 7th. Also in Marché Saint-Honoré. Delicious temptations in a swish designer décor. Fabulous madeleines and seasonal cakes from the talented M Pouget.

La Pâtisserie des Rêves

93 rue du Bac, 75007 Paris
+33 (0)1 42 84 00 82
Métro: Sèvres Babylone
www.lapatisseriedes reves.com
Philippe Conticini displays his amazing contemporary take on patisserie classics in his super colourful modern boutique. Don't miss it!

Carl Marletti

51 rue Censier, 75005 Paris
+33 (0)1 43 31 68 12
Métro: Censier-Daubenton
www.carlmarletti.com
Probably the best *tarte au citron* in Paris at this prize winning patissier who at his enchanting boutique turns out some of the most delectable pastries and chocolates in town.

Jean Millet

103, rue St. Dominque, 75007 Paris
+33 (0)1 45 51 49 80
Métro: École Militaire
A small neighbourhood patisserie with a big following. Great *pain au chocolate* and *tarte au citron*, and some of the best *Mont Blancs* in Paris.

Rollet Pradier

6 rue de Bourgogne, 75007 Paris
+33 (0)1 47 05 77 08
Métro: Assemblée Nationale
www.pradierparis.com
An elegant patisserie, boulangerie and *salon de thé* across the road from the Assemblée Nationale which is a Paris institution serving great classics.

Stohrer

51 rue Montorgueil 75002 Paris
+33 (0)1 42 33 38 20
Métro: Étienne Marcel
www.stohrer.fr
The oldest patisserie in Paris with an enchanting history. Try their famous *baba au rhum*. The éclairs are amazing too!

Vandermeersch

278, avenue Daumesnil, 75012 Paris
+33 (0)1 43 47 21 66
Métro: Porte Dorée
Well worth the ride out to the 12th for a taste of their *millefeuille* or *kugelhopf*. One of the most beautiful pastry shop exteriors in Paris.

SALONS DE THÉ

Angelina

226 rue de Rivoli, 75001 Paris
+33 (0)1 42 60 82 00
Métro: Tuileries
www.angelina-paris.fr
Much has been written about this Paris landmark with its star-studded clientele, eponymous *Mont Blancs*, rich hot chocolate and the gorgeous *belle époque* décor. Get there early if you don't want to queue.

Bonnes Adresses à Paris

Ladurée
16 rue Royale, 75008 Paris
+33 (0)1 42 60 21 79
Métro: Concorde or Madeleine
www.laduree.fr
Visit Ladurée to sample their macarons or other wonderfully indulgent confections. Go and enjoy the fantasy surroundings, beautiful packaging and sense of history. Salons also at *75 Avenue Champs-Elysée, 75008* and *21 rue Bonaparte, 75006*

CONFISERIES

L'Étoile d'Or
30, rue Fontaine, 75009 Paris
+33 (0)1 48 74 59 55
Métro: Blanche
The delightfully eccentric and enthusiastic Denise Acabo will make a trip to this fairy tale sweet shop-cum-chocolatier a visit to remember, as will the Bernachon chocolate and the salted butter caramel spread from Henri Le Roux.

Meert
16 rue Elzévir, 75003 Paris
+33 (0)1 49 96 56 90
Métro: Saint-Paul
www.meert.fr
A long-established *confiserie*-cum-chocolatier from Lille that has opened an old-style shop in the Marais.

Le Bonbon au Palais
19 rue Monge, 75005 Paris
+33 (0)1 78 56 15 72
Métro: Maubert Mutualité
www.bonbonsaupalais.fr
The charming Georges will take you on his trip down memory lane with regional sweets from all over France. Try his pralines from Mazet – the best in France.

GOURMET FOOD SHOPS

Fauchon
24-26 place de la Madeleine, 75008 Paris
+33 (0)1 70 39 38 00
Métro: Madeleine
www.fauchon.com
A trip to this Paris landmark is a culinary adventure, especially their patisserie counter for some of the best macarons and éclairs in Paris. Their delicatessen is amazing too.

Hédiard
21, place de la Madeleine, 75008 Paris
+33 (0)1 43 12 88 88
Métro:Madeleine
www.hediard.com
This flagship store is one of my favourites in Paris… an you will not forget. Their *pate de fruits* are the best in France, so are the *Marron Glacés*. Great for presents!

La Grand Epicerie du Bon Marché
38 rue de Sèvres, 75007 Paris
+33 (0)1 44 39 81 00
Métro: Sèvres Babylone
www.lagrandeepicerie.fr
A great gourmet experience with an excellent patisserie counter and one of the best wine departments in Paris.

CUP CAKERIES

Chloe.S
40 rue Jean-Baptiste Pigalle, 75009 Paris
+33 (0)1 48 78 12 65
Métro: Pigalle
www.cakechloes.com
This fun, playful, all-pink cup cakerie-cum-tea room run by the coquettish Chloe is a must for lovers of these sugary fripperies.

Synie's Cupcakes
23 rue de l'Abbé Grégoire, 75006 Paris
+33 (0)1 45 44 54 23
Métro: Sèvres Babylone or Saint Placide
www.syniescupcakes.com
A really fabulously entertaining and friendly cup cake shop doing delicious stuff, as well as state-of-the-art savoury cup cakes. Give it a try!

USEFUL WEBSITES

www.chloe-chocolat.com
The delightful Chloé Doutre-Roussel is one of the world's leading chocolate experts. Buy some of the most delicious chocolate bars in the world and book a chocolate tour of the best chocolatiers in Paris.

www.davidlebovitz.com
Author, blogger and, passionate foodie American David Lebovitz is the man to follow. His witty advice on where to visit in Paris is invaluable.

Index

....

For Kumiko, my deepest gratitude for your support, love and collaboration

Published in 2012 by Hardie Grant Books

Hardie Grant Books (UK)
Dudley House, North Suite
34–35 Southampton Street
London WC2E 7HF
www.hardiegrant.co.uk

Hardie Grant Books (Australia)
Ground Floor, Building 1
658 Church Street
Melbourne, VIC 3121
www.hardiegrant.com.au

British Library Cataloguing-in-Publication Data. A catalogue
record for this book is available from the British Library.

ISBN 978-174270186-8

Text copyright and photographs © Michael Paul 2012

Commissioning editor: **Kate Pollard**
Design: **David Rowley**
Editor: **Lorraine Jerram**

Colour reproduction by MDP
Printed and bound in China by 1010

10 9 8 7 6 5 4 3

Acknowledgements

*My heartfelt gratitude goes out to everyone who helped in
the crafting of this book. In particular I want to especially
thank Chloé Doutre-Roussel, Stephen and Jane Durbridge,
Paul Bowyer, Luca Selvi and Carla Coulson. I also want to
thank all the owners, pâtissiers, boulangers and chocolatiers
who welcomed my wife and I to their establishments and
allowed us to photograph their art forms. In particular
Apollonia Poilane, Pierre Hermé, Fabrice Le Bourdat,
Gérard Mulot, Patrick Roger, Catherine Cluizel, Sadaharu
Aoki, Claire Damon, Nathalie Robert et Didier Mathray,
Christophe Vasseur, Georges from Le Bonbon au Palais and
Denise Acabo. Also Chloé from Chloé.S and Synie from
Synie's Cupcakes.*

*Above all I want to thank Kumiko for all her
inspiration, support, styling and creativity. Without her this
book would not be possible. Merci beaucoup.*

Notes: In most cases I have used the French names for the
recipes, pastries and desserts – for example, macaron for
macaroon – and the common French terms or translations for
many ingredients, none of which should present any difficulty
for non-French speakers.